A BRIEF
HISTORY
OF THE
AMERICAN
LABOR
MOVEMENT

1970
EDITION
BULLETIN
1000

U.S. DEPARTMENT
OF LABOR
George P. Shultz,
Secretary

BUREAU OF
LABOR STATISTICS
Geoffrey H. Moore,
Commissioner

PREFACE

The *Brief History of the American Labor Movement* introduces readers to the mainstreams of trade unionism in the United States. It will serve its major purpose if it stimulates among readers a deeper interest in the story of American labor and American unions. Detailed histories are listed on the inside back cover of this publication.

This is the fourth edition of the Brief History. The first appeared in 1950. Events that have occurred since 1964, the date of the third edition, have necessitated a recasting of the chapters dealing with post-war developments. Since time lends perspective to all of our activities, future editions of this history will undoubtedly require a new appraisal of recent years.

This revision was prepared in the Bureau of Labor Statistics, Division of Industrial Relations, under the direct supervision of Harry P. Cohany, Chief. Acknowledgment is due to contributors to both the old and new publications, including former and present Bureau of Labor Statistics employees, Theodore W. Reedy, John M. Brumm, Nelson M. Bortz, Witt Bowden, Joseph W. Bloch, and Professor Albert A. Blum of Michigan State University.

CONTENTS

CONTENTS.. Continued

Page

Part of the mural in the lobby of the AFL-CIO building in Washington, D.C.

CHAPTER I

EARLY ORGANIZATION

Unions have a long history in the United States. Even before the Declaration of Independence, skilled artisans in handicraft and domestic industry joined together in benevolent societies, primarily to provide members and their families with financial assistance in the event of serious illness, debt, or death of the wage earner. Although these early associations had few of the characteristics of present-day labor unions, they did bring workers together to consider problems of mutual concern and to devise ways and means for their solution.

Early Local Craft Unions

Crafts such as those of carpenters, shoemakers, and printers formed separate organizations in Philadelphia, New York, and Boston as early as 1791, largely to resist wage reductions. These unions were confined to local areas and were usually weak because they seldom included all the workers of a craft. Generally, they continued in existence for only a short time. In addition to the welfare activities, these unions frequently sought higher wages, minimum rates, shorter hours, enforcement of apprenticeship regulations, and establishment of the principle of exclusive union hiring, later known as the "closed shop."

Many characteristic union techniques were first developed in this period. The first recorded meeting of worker and employer representatives for discussion of labor demands occurred between the Philadelphia shoemakers and their employers in 1799. The printing crafts of Philadelphia and New York rapidly followed suit.

TRIAL

OF TWENTY-FOUR

JOURNEYMEN TAILORS,

CHARGED WITH A

CONSPIRACY:

BEFORE

THE MAYOR'S COURT

OF THE CITY OF

PHILADELPHIA,

September Sessions, 1827.

REPORTED BY

MARCUS T. C. GOULD,

Stenographer.

PHILADELPHIA:

1827.

The courts came to the defense of early 19th-century employers by charging the new unions with conspiracy in restraint of trade.

A forerunner of the union business agent grew out of the need to check on shops to see whether they were adhering to the union wage scale. The early "tramping committees" and unpaid representatives later led to specialized, paid agents known as "walking delegates."

Strikes, during which workmen quit their employment in a body, paralleled the development of organization and collective bargaining. The New York bakers were said to have stopped work to enforce their demands as early as 1741, although this action was directed more against the local government, which set the price of bread, than against the employers. The first authenticated strike was called in 1768 by the New York tailors to protest a reduction in wages. A sympathetic strike of shoe workers in support of fellow bootmakers occurred in 1799 in Philadelphia. In 1805, the shoemakers of New York created a "permanent" strike benefit fund, and in 1809, these same workers participated in what was perhaps the first multiemployer strike when they extended strike action against one employer to include several others who had come to his aid.

Employer Opposition

As unions became stronger, the wage question increased in importance and employers organized to resist wage demands. Where circumstances appeared favorable, employers attempted to destroy the effectiveness of a union by hiring nonunion workers and by appealing to the courts to declare the labor organization illegal. The legal fight against unions was carried through the courts in Philadelphia, New York, and Pittsburgh between 1806 and 1814. Unions were prosecuted as "conspiracies in restraint of trade" under an old English common law doctrine that combinations of workmen to raise wages could be regarded as a conspiracy against the public.

The attempt of courts to apply this conspiracy doctrine aroused a controversy which lasted throughout most of the nineteenth century. Slowly, judicial attention was shifted from the question as to whether a mere combination of workmen was a conspiracy to one as to the means they used to gain their ends. Thus while unions, as such, became regarded as "lawful," strikes, boycotts, and other attempts of workers to secure their demands were the subject of legal action in the courts for many decades.

The early conspiracy cases, combined with a business recession following the Napoleonic wars in Europe, seriously affected the trade unions, many of which passed out of existence. After a low point in membership in 1820, however, worker organizations again sprang up in the larger cities among hatters, tailors, weavers, nailers, and cabinetmakers. Organizations of factory workers also appeared for the first time during this period.

Early Efforts of Unions in Politics

Between 1827 and 1832, workers' organizations gradually turned to independent political activity. The factors leading to this development are explained by the historian, Mary Beard, who, in *A Short History of the American Labor Movement,* says:

> In the first place, property qualifications on the right to vote, which had been imposed by the first State constitutions, were abandoned and the ballot put into the hands of practically every workingman. In the second place, the prosecutions of labor unions in the courts of law had driven workingmen to a concerted action which rose above trade and craft lines. In the third place, the industrial revolution brought about by steam-power and the factory system was making swift headway in creating great cities. It added rapidly to the number of industrial workers and created closer associations among them. In the fourth place, the idea was being advanced that the hours of labor should be fixed universally at 10 per day by legislation rather than by the painful method of strike.

This movement among workers seeking to improve their status by political action spread to many leading industrial communities. In Philadelphia a number of craft unions formed the Mechanics' Union of Trade Associations in 1827. This citywide group soon began to nominate and elect candidates to "represent the interests of the working classes" in the Philadelphia city council and the Pennsylvania State Legislature. Local labor parties organized by workers also sprang up in many States.

Political programs, supported by 50 or more labor papers, included such demands as the following: The 10-hour day, restriction of child labor, abolition of convict labor competition, free and equal public education, abolition of imprisonment for debt, exemption of wages and tools from seizure for debt, the right of mechanics to file liens on property to secure payment of their wages, and the abolition of home and factory sweatshops.

For a short time, these labor organizations were successful in electing their candidates to various public offices, but in general, they failed to attain their aims. Nevertheless, they called the attention of the regular political parties and the public at large to the social and economic inequalities experienced by workers and by so doing helped to shape the course of much future legislation. Eventually, State legislatures prohibited imprisonment for debt, enacted the 10-hour day for women and children, and laid the foundation of the American free public school system.

Formation of City Centrals and National Unions

In the early 1830's, the interest of workers in reform movements and political action declined. To offset the rapidly rising prices between 1835 and 1837, they turned with renewed vigor to the organization of craft or trade unions. By 1836, for example, over 50 local unions were active in Philadelphia and New York City. Workers also organized craft unions in other cities, such as Newark, Boston, Cincinnati, Pittsburgh, and Louisville. This rapid growth led to the formation of union groups on a citywide basis. These "city central" organizations, or "trades' unions," as they were called at the time, gave primary attention to the discussion of problems of common interest and to the promotion of union-made goods.

Organizations of union groups beyond a single local area began to emerge. In 1834, city central bodies from seven cities met in New York to form the National Trades' Union. Later, in 1835 and 1836, the cordwainers, typographers, combmakers, carpenters, and hand-loom weavers endeavored to set up countrywide organizations of their separate crafts. These experiments in federation, however, did not withstand the financial panic of 1837 and the period of depression and unemployment which followed during most of the forties.

The Era of "Utopianism"

As the depression of the 1840's took its toll of local as well as national unions, workmen in many places turned their efforts toward forming producers' and consumers' cooperatives. Others were attracted by various schemes for cooperative communities stimulated by the "utopian" ideas spread by the followers of the French Socialist Charles Fourier, by the English reformer Robert Owen, and my many other intellectuals of the period.

Community ownership of land and productive tools, like that tried in the well-known Brook Farm venture in Massachusetts and at the New Harmony colony in Indiana, was urged as the solution to poverty, unemployment, and the other social and economic ills besetting labor. Although widely discussed in labor groups, these schemes received little direct support from workers themselves. However, they did divert some workers' efforts from union activities into disputes over political and economic theories.

In this period, also, the "homestead movement" was born. This proposal authorized the Government to give plots of undeveloped public land to persons for settlement and cultivation. This movement, according to Selig Perlman in *A History of Trade Unionism in the United States,* had as one of its goals that the Government "open an escape to the worker from the wage system into self-employment by way of free land."

An Unsettled Decade

By the late 1840's, industry had revived, labor was in great demand, prices were climbing upward, and trade unions once more showed signs of activity. Workingmen again focused attention on establishing rules governing apprenticeship, minimum wage scales, control over methods of wage payment, initiation fees, dues, strike benefit funds, union hiring procedures, the closed shop, and the exclusion from membership of all persons not working at the trade. As industries spread, new locals were formed and by 1854 most important trades showed some degree of organization in the larger cities. Many of these unions collapsed only to be promptly revived and crushed again in 1857 in another downward sweep of the business cycle.

During the 1850's, several national unions were founded. The Printers' Union held a national convention in 1850. By 1859, the Stonecutters, Hat Finishers, Molders, Machinists, and Locomotive Engineers also had created national organizations. The decade was marked by many strikes which, at one time or another, involved almost every known craft and most American cities. Collective bargaining between unions and management, however, was slowly becoming more prevalent in several leading trades.

By 1860, there was a definite trend toward higher wages and shorter hours for workers. Adequate data are lacking to prove that this trend was a direct result of union activity. However, scattered bits of evidence indicate that the combined efforts of workers were responsible for at least a part of the improvement in working conditions. For example, a letter written by President Martin Van Buren in 1840 to certain political inquirers states that: "The 10-hour system, originally devised by the mechanics and laborers themselves, has by my direction been adopted and uniformly carried out at all public establishments." A report of the Massachusetts Legislature for 1850 also tells that "the mechanics and laboring people have established by mutual arrangement with their employers the '10-hour system' of labor."

Specifically, the workday, often from sunrise to sunset early in the century, was shortened to 10 hours for most skilled artisans in the large cities by 1850. At that time, factory workers worked from 11 to 12 hours a day. By 1860, the average workday for nonagricultural employees was estimated at 11 hours, while the building trades averaged about 10 hours. Wages, which ranged in 1820 from 75 cents to $1.25 a day for common labor, depending upon the locality and season, were from $1 to $1.25 a day in 1850. Wages of more skilled artisans and mechanics in the cities similarly advanced from $1.25 and $1.50 a day in 1820 to between $1.50 and $2 or more by 1860.

Emergence of National Unions

The armed conflict between the Northern and Southern States (1861–65) required large quantities of munitions and other factory goods. Prices rose, profits were large, and many new industries were started during this period of civil war. New railroads brought the country closer together. Factory goods from Massachusetts, New York, and other Eastern

States were shipped by rail to the West. Other factories were built in the cities emerging along the Great Lakes and down the Mississippi Valley.

Unions sought to organize the skilled workers employed by these new enterprises. In 1863, there were approximately 80 local unions in 20 Northern States; by 1864, these States had almost 300 local unions. City centrals (local federations) followed soon after the organization of local unions. A short-lived effort toward a countrywide labor federation was made in 1864 when several of these city centrals established the International Industrial Assembly of North America. National and international unions [1] developed more slowly but steadily year by year; 13 appeared between 1861 and 1865. The unions formed in these years became relatively strong and permanent organizations which in a few cases (the plasterers, cigarmakers, bricklayers, and masons) have continued to the present day.

The 15 years following the Civil War was an important formative period for the American labor movement. During 2 cycles of economic recession and revival, 14 new national unions were formed. Union membership rose to 300,000 by 1872, and then dropped to 50,000 by 1878. Three unsuccessful attempts were made to unite the various craft organizations into national labor federations. This period also marked the rise of the 8-hour-day movement and the first signs of the long, bitter, and sometimes violent industrial warfare which characterized the struggle of American unionism for recognition and survival.

Establishment of the National Labor Union (NLU) in Baltimore in 1866 was a response to a growing demand for unification of labor groups throughout the country. Basically

[1] Unions first called themselves "international" when some of the affiliated locals were outside the United States, usually in Canada. Today, the terms "national unions" and "international unions" are used interchangeably.

a loose federation of city centrals, it included also national and local unions and various social reform organizations. Although one of the purposes of its founders had been to encourage industrial peace through the promotion of collective bargaining, the National Labor Union soon veered from "pure" trade unionism. After first concentrating on the 8-hour-day movement, it later tried to stimulate a revival of labor interest in producers' cooperatives.

The driving personality behind the NLU was William H. Sylvis, of the Molders' Union, who believed in cooperation as a means of freeing workers from the "control" of capitalism. The example of cooperative production undertaken by Sylvis' own union was followed on a limited scale by others, such as the bakers, shipwrights, machinists, tailors, and printers. Because such cooperative enterprise required capital and credit, the NLU was prompted to support the various politically inclined farm groups in the "Greenback" movement which favored large issues of paper money and easy credit at low interest rates.

The year 1872 saw the end of the NLU after its brief and rapid evolution from trade unionism to a body which sponsored cooperatives and supported political groups. The National Reform and Labor Party, which it sponsored in 1872, failed to survive even one election, and by the end of the seventies few of its cooperatives remained. However, the emphasis which the NLU had placed on State and Federal legislation had borne some fruit. In 1868, Congress established an 8-hour day for Federal employees. A Federal Bureau of Labor, which had been advocated by the NLU, was provided by law in 1884. Originally named the Bureau of Labor, this Federal agency evolved into the present Bureau of Labor Statistics of the U.S. Department of Labor.

Industrial Strife

In 1873 and again in 1876, several leading craft unions attempted unsuccessfully to revive interest in a federation based on a strictly trade union program. Trade union membership, meanwhile, was being seriously reduced by a new economic depression. Industrial workers were involved in a series of violent strikes and lockouts which their organizations were financially too weak to endure. The cigarmakers, textile workers, ironworkers, coal miners, and others fought bitterly against wage reductions.

In 1877, the railroad strikes, which originated in Pittsburgh but spread throughout the country, produced riots, martial law, intervention of State and Federal troops, and some fatalities. A notorious secret association known as the "Molly Maguires" gained control of lodges of the Ancient Order of Hibernians in the anthracite regions of Pennsylvania. A product of the distress and poverty of this period, the "Molly Maguires" used terroristic methods against employers and strikebreakers. This group was finally broken up by State authorities when several ringleaders were arrested, charged with a series of murders, and convicted.

Despite the failure of workers to win their immediate objectives, this turbulent period brought a growing recognition of the nationwide significance of the labor movement and of the social and economic ills which it was attempting to remedy. Selig Perlman observed that the experience of these years "nationalized" the labor movement, developing within it a consciousness of solidarity and common purpose. For the first time, also, unskilled workers—on the railroads, in the mines, in the textile mills—played a significant role in industrial conflict, and the organized labor movement was no longer identified exclusively with the craft groups. Although unions continued to represent mainly the skilled, the semiskilled and unskilled did not join to any vast extent until the New Deal period in the 1930's.

When economic conditions improved, new locals of skilled workers appeared and new city centrals were formed because few of the old had survived the depression. Some 18 national unions had survived; 9 others were soon established. By 1885, total union membership again reached the 300,000 level in spite of the economic recession beginning in 1883 which had brought on a wave of strikes against wage reductions.

During the union-employer struggles of this decade, the labor movement itself became the scene of a decisive contest over its future structure. The Knights of Labor championed a nationwide organization of labor based upon the direct affiliation of local unions and city centrals cutting across trade lines. This approach had been tried unsuccessfully several times. After its founding in the 1880's, the American Federation of Labor favored a national federation based primarily on existing national trade or craft unions.

CHAPTER II

DEVELOPMENT OF THE MODERN LABOR MOVEMENT

Labor's past has been a prelude to its present. The growth and development of the modern labor movement is an oft-repeated story of inter- and intra-union squabbles, sometimes bloody clashes between the organizers and management, and continuing political activity by organized labor. On the other hand, differences within the labor movement have led to unique organizations to pursue labor's goals and philosophies. Just as the Noble Order of the Knights of Labor had within it the seeds of the American Federation of Labor, the AFL had within it another rival group (chapter III).

The Knights of Labor

The Noble Order of the Knights of Labor was founded by Uriah S. Stephens in 1869 as a small local union of Philadelphia garment workers. It expanded slowly as various other craft unions joined. For some years it functioned as a secret society with an elaborate ritual, a practice best understood in the light of the difficulties experienced by unions at the time when, as one contemporary labor leader wrote, "a great deal of bitterness was evinced against trade union organizations, and men were blacklisted to an extent hardly ever equaled." Most of the secrecy, however, was abandoned by 1881.

From an estimated membership of 10,000 in 1879, the Knights of Labor grew rapidly until by 1886 it claimed over 700,000 members throughout the country. Structurally, the Knights consisted of a national body or general assembly exercising centralized control over numerous district assem-

blies, each of which was composed of five or more local
assemblies. Local assemblies were of two kinds, trade and
mixed. The former included members of only one craft while
the latter admitted a wide range of occupations and professions. The first general assembly, called in 1878, elected
Stephens as Grand Master Workman. He resigned shortly
thereafter and was succeeded by Terence V. Powderly.

*Frank J. Farrell introduces Terence V. Powderly, the "Gen-
eral Master Workman," to the 10th annual convention of
the Knights of Labor, held in Richmond, Va.*

The Order had a broad aim: the replacement of a competitive society by a cooperative one which would give workers the opportunity to enjoy fully the wealth they created. This was to be achieved primarily through reducing the "money power" of banks, not through battles with individual employers. More concretely, the Knights' program called for the 8-hour day, equal pay for equal work by women, abolition of convict and child labor, public ownership of utilities, and the establishment of cooperatives. Reliance was placed on educational and political methods rather than on collective bargaining. Strikes were to be employed only as a last resort.

During the eighties, however, when the "practical trade unionist" forces gained influence, the Knights engaged in a series of strikes for better wages and made wage agreements with employers. Their most successful struggle, with the powerful Gould railway system in 1885, brought them particular prestige.

An internal conflict led to the decline of the Knights of Labor. Leaders who favored processes of collective bargaining clashed with those committed to political means and basic social change. Moreover, the immediate interests of the skilled and unskilled workers whom the Knights attempted to unite were not so easily reconciled. The stronger craft unions resisted affiliation and by 1886 came into open rivalry with the Knights of Labor.

After formation of the American Federation of Labor (AFL), the Knights steadily lost ground. In 1890, the Knights reported only 100,000 members. Thereafter, the Order continued to lose members and ceased to be an influential factor in the labor movement, although continuing in existence until 1917.

The American Federation of Labor

By 1881, the nucleus of a new organization had taken shape. Devoted to "pure and simple unionism," its main goals were higher wages and improved working conditions. The craft unions surviving the depression of 1873 were absorbed almost exclusively in problems of their respective trades. Many of these unions developed strong, centralized, national organizations supported by an increasing number of local lodges. Benefit funds also were collected to assist their members or their families during strikes and times of financial stress due to unemployment, injury, or death.

In 1881, six prominent craft unions—those of the printers, iron and steelworkers, molders, cigarmakers, carpenters and glassworkers—and a variety of other labor groups met in Pittsburgh and established the Federation of Organized Trades and Labor Unions (FOTLU). Its leaders were Samuel Gompers and Adolph Strasser, both of the cigarmakers' union. At the start, the Federation had approximately 45,000 members; for 5 years it remained weak and was overshadowed by the Knights of Labor.

When the Knights at their annual convention in 1886 refused to agree to respect the jurisdiction of the large craft unions, several of the latter met at Columbus, Ohio, and founded the American Federation of Labor. The FOTLU, also in convention at Columbus, amalgamated with the new group. Gompers was elected first president of the new Federation, a position he held, except for 1 year (1894–95), until his death in 1924.

The strength of the AFL resided primarily in the unions of carpenters, cigarmakers, printers, iron and steelworkers, and iron molders. It began with a membership of about 138,000 in 1886 and slowly doubled that number during the next 12 years.

Membership Growth, 1890–1920

In the three decades following 1890, the AFL consolidated its position as the principal federation of American unions.

The first decade of growth was slow, but from 1900 to 1904 membership rose rapidly, from half a million to a million and a half, and then increased irregularly to 2 million by the out-break of World War I. During and immediately following the

The first Labor Day parade, in New York City, on September 5, 1882.

war years, membership again rose rapidly and reached more than 4 million in 1920.

During this entire period, an estimated 70 to 80 percent of all union workers were in the American Federation of Labor. The most important unaffiliated group of unions was the four "railroad brotherhoods" which usually maintained friendly relations with the AFL affiliates. The other non-affiliated unions were a mixed group. They frequently were rivals of the AFL unions. Some were AFL secessionist groups. Membership among this "independent" or unaffiliated group rose from approximately 240,000 in 1900 to almost a million in 1920, according to estimates Leo Wolman made for the National Bureau of Economic Research.

Before World War I, the principal union gains had occurred in the coal mining, railroad, and building trades unions. The most important union of coal miners was the United Mine Workers, an industrial union which, after a strike in 1902, established itself as the largest and one of the most completely organized affiliates of the AFL. In other industries, organizations of crafts or amalgamated crafts still largely prevailed.

Renewed Industrial Conflict

The emergence of the labor movement as an influential national economic group did not occur without opposition or setbacks. In the 1890's, large corporations which had appeared on the economic scene vigorously fought the efforts to unionize their employees. At times, these clashes resulted in violence, injuries, and even death. For example, the unsuccessful struggle of the Amalgamated Association of Iron and Steel Workers against the Carnegie Steel Co. at Homestead, Pa., in 1892 was climaxed by a pitched battle between company-imported Pinkerton detectives and strikers. Before the National Guard intervened to restore order, 10 deaths resulted.

The strike of the American Railway Union led by Eugene V. Debs against the Pullman Palace Parlor Car Co. at Pullman, Ill., in 1894 provoked sympathetic walkouts on many railroads serving the Chicago area. Federal and State troops were used and court injunctions were obtained against

Pinkerton agents, hired by the Carnegie Steel Co., battling with strikers at the company's Homestead, Pa., plant in July 1892. The strike was broken when the company brought in 2,000 strikebreakers protected by the State militia.

the union. Twenty-five persons were killed and 60 were injured during this controversy. Elsewhere in the country industrial disputes sporadically flared into open violence.

After 1902, following a period of rapid union growth, employer opposition stiffened and became more highly organized. Carroll Daugherty, in summarizing this trend in his book *Labor Problems in American Industry,* wrote:

> Most of the powerful ones [employers], believing that unionism was growing too strong and fearing further encroachments on their control of industry, decided to break off relations, and the years from 1902 to World War I were characterized by a definitely increasing antiunionism.

Daugherty then added:

> Scientific management and "efficiency" systems were introduced in many plants, much to the discomfiture of many skilled craft unions. A variety of union-smashing tactics were adopted by employers. Vigilante groups and citizens' committees were fostered to resist unionization activities. Court decisions upheld as a rule most of the employers' antiunion practices. In the face of these new difficulties, the membership of the AFL at first fell off a little and then resumed growth at a much slower rate than before 1902.

However, despite general employer opposition to unions an increasing number of "trade" or collective bargaining agreements were resulting from direct negotiations between unions and employers. The stabilization of industrial relations and the attainment of job security are considered by many authorities as important factors in the success of AFL trade unionism at that period.

Labor's "Nonpartisan" Politics

Between 1900 and the beginning of the First World War, unions concentrated on raising wages, establishing the 8-hour workday, and securing other improvements in working conditions through collective bargaining. On the whole, they resisted the efforts of various political forces in the labor movement to obtain union support for partisan programs. The political role of organized labor was debated in various conventions of the AFL at the turn of the century when, according to Lewis Lorwin, "The principle of nonpartisan politics, summed up in the dictum 'to defeat labor's enemies and to reward its friends,' received official sanction." The AFL's political program was mainly focused on issues which affected only workers and as a body rejected arguments which required its commitment to broad social or political reforms. In practice, these principles meant that the AFL opposed any "independent labor party" but officially supported measures and candidates of the regular political parties favorable to the interests of labor. The AFL continued to be particularly active in city and State politics by acting through State federations and city centrals.

As a consequence, labor was frequently successful in obtaining legislative reforms. During the first two decades of the century, for example, a number of States passed laws regulating the employment of women and children in industry and providing for protection against industrial hazards. Most States adopted workmen's compensation laws. In 1913, the U.S. Congress created a separate Department of Labor.

Clauses inserted in the Clayton Anti-Trust Act of 1914, at the insistence of the AFL, exempted unions from prosecution on the ground of engaging in restraint of trade and sought to limit the issuance of injunctions by Federal courts in labor disputes. This law was hailed by Samuel Gompers and others as the "Magna Carta" of labor. Enthusiasm over the Clayton Act was short lived, however, since subsequent court interpretations virtually nullified labor's anticipated gains. In 1915, Congress passed the Seamen's Act, regulating many of the conditions of employment for American sailors; the Lloyd-La Follette Act, giving public employees the right of lobbying and affiliating with labor organizations;

and, in 1916, enacted the Adamson Act, establishing a basic 8-hour workday for railroad workers engaged in interstate commerce.

Radical Opposition

Although the AFL under Samuel Gompers' leadership was successfully developing along the lines of "pure and simple" unionism, a series of unions, more or less revolutionary in character, rose to challenge it. These unions were committed to the doctrine that labor was engaged in a class struggle, and that a political or revolutionary offensive was the best way to advance the interests of labor. On the other hand, the AFL championed the philosophy that gradual improvement of the economic condition of the worker was the only useful course of action to follow, and that collective bargaining was the chief tool to use. After a long struggle, which continued from the 1890's to the First World War, the philosophy of the AFL clearly emerged as the expressed views of the great majority of the country's organized workers.

Opposition to the strict trade union policies of the AFL unions came from the Socialist Labor Party, the Socialist Party, and the Industrial Workers of the World (IWW). The Socialist Labor Party (SLP), founded in 1874, was a product of the American section of Marx and Engel's International Workingman's Association, or "First International," formed in 1864. This group attempted in 1895 to form a rival body to the AFL—the Socialist Trades and Labor Alliance. Those within the SLP who believed in winning workers to socialist philosophy without resort to "dual unionism" broke away in 1901 and formed the Socialist Party whose members then sought, unsuccessfully, to change traditional AFL policies from within the Federation.

The Industrial Workers of the World was formed in 1905 by several dissident union and political groups. It was pledged to the "abolition of the wage system" and to the organization of the great mass of unskilled factory workers and of migratory or "casual" laborers. The IWW organized workers primarily on an industrial basis and was partly successful for a limited period in some areas throughout the country, notably in the wheat fields, mines, and lumber camps of the West as well as in a few other scattered areas of industrial tension. The militant tactics used to press its demands, particularly during the First World War, brought the IWW into public disfavor and caused several States to outlaw the organization. Many of its leaders were prosecuted and sentenced to long terms in prison. Once considered a possible contender to the AFL for supremacy in the labor movement, the IWW declined rapidly after America's entry into World War I.

Striking Transport Workers in 1966 get picket line support from Communication Workers of America in New York City.

Labor and the First World War

During World War I, increased industrial activity and labor shortages brought a rapid expansion of unions. A National War Labor Board was created to promote union-management cooperation and to aid in 'the settlement of serious disputes which might interfere with the effective conduct of the war. For the first time in the history of the country, a Federal labor agency set forth the right of workers to organize in trade unions and encouraged collective bargaining with employers through chosen representatives.

In addition to serving on the National War Labor Board, representatives from organized labor participated on other Government boards and committees dealing with specialized war problems. Their cooperation with Government, on a scale theretofore unprecedented, secured for labor a hearing on specific complaints about industrial conditions as well as a voice in the determination of broad national issues.

Union membership increased in the mining and shipbuilding industries, and also on the railroads, which were operated by the Federal Government during the war. Notable gains were made also in the packinghouse, textile, men's clothing, food and leather, and metal trades industries. Large groups of semiskilled and unskilled workers were, for the first time, brought within the trade union movement.

As a result of organizing activity in the favorable climate of Federal protection, union membership increased to more than 5 million by 1920.

More important than the numerical gain in union membership were the economic gains made by the workers, particularly during the years of, and immediately following, the First World War. Average hourly earnings in all manufacturing industries, which were about 15 cents in 1890, rose slowly to 22 cents in 1914, then jumped to 47 cents in 1919. In 1923, they were about 52 cents. At the same time, average hours worked per week in all manufacturing declined from more than 60 in 1890 to 49 in 1914. In 1923, the average workweek approximated 46 hours.

CHAPTER III

BETWEEN TWO WORLD WARS

During the year following World War I, a combination of events occurred which led to an increase in the number and severity of industrial disputes. Following a brief downswing in business immediately after the war, there was a quick revival, accompanied by rising prices. By mid-1919, labor was faced with the mounting cost of living. Real wages lagged. At the same time, withdrawal of the Government's limited protection of labor's right to organize and the termination of wartime governmental labor agencies removed restraints which had kept industrial relations running more or less smoothly during the war years. As a result, numerous employers refused to recognize labor unions which had been organized in their plants. So, to protect their recently won gains, and to combat the victories of antiunion employers many labor leaders called for more aggressive action.

Open Shop Era and Depression

In September 1919, a strike was called in the steel industry by the AFL Iron and Steel Organizing Committee composed of the presidents of the 24 international unions that had jurisdiction in the industry. The strike was called off in January 1920, after most of the strikers had drifted back to work; the unions failed in their attempts to gain recognition in the industry. A strike by the United Mine Workers in the coal-mining industry began on October 31, 1919, but was called off on November 10 after the court granted the Government a permanent injunction against it. In some localities, the strike continued into December 1919, when the union agreed to the Fuel Administrator's proposal for an immediate 14-percent wage increase and to President

Woodrow Wilson's offer to appoint a tripartite coal commission to pass on further demands.

The economic recession in 1921 and 1922 resulted in many serious work stoppages, such as the railroad shopmen's strike in the summer of 1922. These protests, however, failed to check a general wage reduction movement which also marked the beginning of a decline in union strength. Many unions continued to lose ground despite the rise in business activity which occurred in the late 1920's. Professors Millis and Montgomery in their book *Organized Labor* advised that the 1920's were years which should "according to historical precedents, have witnessed labor militancy, aggressiveness in conquering unorganized areas, and in entrenching more strongly job control already obtained." Instead, this period "found old and established unions experiencing difficulty in maintaining past gains and something akin to inertia, pacifism, or disillusionment pervading the movement as a whole."

The successes of antiunion employers in many industries (metal, automobile, railroad, etc.) gave this period its popular title—the "open shop era." To weaken or disrupt labor organizations employers in these years introduced a variety of welfare measures, ranging from athletic fields to pension plans, as well as such repressive measures as the use of spies and strikebreakers. Company unions dominated by employers were likewise established. "Yellow dog" contracts, requiring a worker to promise, as a condition of employment, that he would not join a labor union, were also used effectively.

The varied effects of this period on the union movement are described by Lewis Lorwin in his book *The American Federation of Labor:*

> A considerable part of the membership was able to obtain higher wage rates, increased earnings, and shorter hours. The 40-hour week in unionized plants was widely accepted, while about half a million union members obtained the 5-day week. This was notable in the building trades, in some branches

of the transportation industry, in the printing trades, in Government employment, and in some of the professions, such as teaching and acting. But where unions were unable to meet the new conditions they suffered a decline in membership, a loss of income, and a weakening of their benefit systems; and they could enforce their standards over smaller areas.

From 1920 to 1923, total union membership fell from about 5 million to slightly over 3½ million. It still remained at this lower level (approximately 3,625,000) in 1929, at the height of the country's "prosperity." Of the 105 AFL international and national unions active in 1929, only 44 had held their own or expanded their membership after 1925. Most of these were in the building and printing trades, transportation, Government service, and amusements.

The economic depression and widespread unemployment which followed the 1929 stockmarket crash further reduced union membership to 3¼ million by 1932. This decline was particularly pronounced in industries where machinery was displacing skilled hand labor and in the "sick" industries of mining and textiles, as well as in other industries which had been artificially stimulated by the war. Many unions were hardpressed to survive and maintain some semblance of effectiveness.

New Labor Laws

Although the decline in union membership was a serious blow to the labor movement, about 3 million workers retained their membership during the depth of the depression. These workers provided the vital centers of growth ready to respond to improved economic conditions, especially when many of the obstacles to union growth were removed by changes in public policies.

The Railway Labor Act of 1926, although limited to railroad transportation, was a significant beginning of these new policies. This act was based on the premise that peaceful

labor-management relations should be maintained by free
collective bargaining between employers and unions. Railroad
workers were assured the right to organize and join unions
without employer interference. As a measure drafted by representatives of the railroad companies and the unions, the
1926 law has been described as "in effect a collective agreement sanctioned by Congress." Another act indicative of the
new trend was the Davis-Bacon Act of 1931. Not so directly
related to collective bargaining, this act determined the prevailing rates of pay for workers engaged in the construction
of public works paid from Federal funds.

Next came the Norris-LaGuardia Act of 1932. It brought
to an end what has been called, in the history of labor-
management relations, the era of "government by injunction." It drastically limited judicial restrictions on strikes,
picketing, and boycotts. The act also forbade the use of
the "yellow dog" contract whereby workers, as a condition
of employment, would agree not to join a union, and it
limited the liability of unions and their officers and members
for unlawful acts of individual officers, agents, or members.

A year later, in an effort to revive business and reduce
widespread unemployment, the incoming Franklin 'D. Roosevelt Administration obtained the passage of the National
Industrial Recovery Act (NIRA) in the spring of 1933. This
law included a provision, section 7 (a), which guaranteed
the right of employees to organize or join unions of their
own choosing and to bargain collectively with their employers. The NIRA was invalidated by the Supreme Court
in May 1935, but in July of the same year the principle of
the labor section was incorporated in the National Labor
Relations (Wagner) Act.

The Wagner Act was the most significant labor law thus
far enacted in the United States. It guaranteed employees
"the right to self-organization, to form, join, or assist labor
organizations, to bargain collectively through representatives
of their own choosing, and to engage in concerted activities
for the purpose of collective bargaining or other mutual aid

or protection." The act went beyond a statement of principles; it created the administrative machinery of the National Labor Relations Board. As a Government agency, the Board was given, among other duties, the following functions: (1) To prevent and remedy employers' "unfair labor practices" which discouraged or interfered with the self-organization of employees or with the practice of collective bargaining; and (2) to determine the bargaining unit in cases of controversy and hold secret "representation" elections to decide which union, if any, the employees wanted to represent them for bargaining purposes, and with which the company, by law, had to bargain collectively.

This trend toward a more favorable Government policy was undoubtedly one of the main causes of the success of unions in the organizing work which followed in the mid-thirties. This Government attitude was also reflected in the enactment of measures other than those for regulating labor-management relations, such as the principle of minimum wage and maximum hours standards of the National Industrial Recovery Act, later reflected in the Fair Labor Standards (Wage-Hour) Act of 1938; the Social Security Act (1935); the Walsh-Healey (Public Contracts) Act (1936) for maintaining basic labor standards for materials or supplies furnished on Federal contracts exceeding $10,000; and improved State workmen's compensation laws.

Revival of Unionism

Increases in union membership following the enactment of the Norris-LaGuardia Act in 1932 and the National Industrial Recovery Act in the spring of 1933 were most conspicuous in the mass-production industries. New unions in these industries were organized on an industrial rather than a craft basis. No corresponding international unions existed to absorb them, and they were therefore chartered directly by the AFL as federal labor unions. Many of the older national and international unions made large gains in membership during the same period. Growth was slowed down to some extent by the widespread increase in the formation of "employee representation plans" sponsored by employers mainly to check the spread of unions. The Wagner Act, however, established a basic code to encourage free collective bargaining and virtually ended company-dominated unions and employer-controlled employee representation plans.

The 2-year expansion of total union membership brought about a rise from less than 3 million in 1933 to 3¾ million in 1935. In the following 2 years (the first 2 years of the Wagner Act), membership almost doubled, advancing to 7¼ million. The largest gains during the latter period were made in the automobile, rubber, and aluminum industries, in which workers were organized on an industrial basis. Many of the older organizations, including such unions as the International Ladies' Garment Workers' Union, the International Association of Machinists, and the International Brotherhood of Teamsters, Chauffeurs, Warehousemen and Helpers, also registered substantial membership increases. The extent of these gains is even more impressive when it is realized that the total labor force increased only 2 percent between 1935 and 1937, and that nonagricultural employment, the main source of union membership, increased less than 15 percent.

Division in the Labor Movement

Growth in union membership was accomplished even though an internal struggle developed in the American Federation of Labor, primarily over the question of whether unions should be organized to include all workers in an industry, or strictly on a craft or occupational basis. The San Francisco (1934) convention of the American Federation of Labor unanimously adopted a report of its resolutions committee which declared that in the mass-production industries new methods had been developed for organizing workers who were "most difficult or impossible to organize into craft unions." The report continued:

> To meet this new condition, the Executive Council is directed to issue charters to national and international unions in the automotive, cement, aluminum and such other mass-production and miscellaneous industries as in the judgment of the Executive Council may be necessary to meet the situation.

The resolution also stated that the jurisdictional rights of existing trade unions would be recognized. Craft unions would continue in those industries where skills and work assignments were distinguishable among crafts.

During the following year, the American Federation of Labor granted charters to organizations of workers in the automobile and rubber industries. In defining the jurisdiction of these unions, however, the AFL Executive Council excluded certain skilled craftsmen and maintenance employees coming under the jurisdiction of other unions.

The industrial or craft organization issue, however, was not to be settled that easily. It rose again at the AFL's Atlantic City (1935) convention. A minority report of the resolutions committee protested the Executive Council's interpretation of the San Francisco declaration on industrial unionism and called for the granting of "unrestricted charters" to organizations set up in mass-production industries. Defeat of the minority report by a vote of 18,024 to 10,093, after lengthy debate, left the issue unresolved and led to the schism in the labor movement which lasted until December 1955.

Formation of Committee for Industrial Organization

A few weeks after the 1935 convention, six AFL affiliated unions and the officers of two other AFL unions formed a "Committee for Industrial Organization (CIO)." Its stated purpose was to promote the organization of workers in mass-production and unorganized industries and to encourage their affiliation with the American Federation of Labor. The committee was later joined by four additional AFL unions.[2]

The Executive Council of the American Federation of Labor characterized the activities of the Committee for Industrial Organization as "dual" to the AFL and in January 1936 requested the committee to disband immediately. The CIO rejected the request. The "dual" unions were suspended later in the year. Efforts at compromise and conciliation failed, and in May 1938 all but one of the unions in the committee were expelled. The lone exception was the International Ladies' Garment Workers' Union (ILGWU), which had remained friendly to the Federation and which had attempted to bring the disputing factions together. The ILGWU rejoined the AFL in 1940.

The CIO held its first constitutional convention in Pittsburgh, Pa., in November 1938. At this convention, the Committee for Industrial Organization was reorganized as a federation of national and international unions under the name "Congress of Industrial Organizations." The new federation included the 9 unions expelled from the AFL and

[2] The unions active in the formation of the CIO were: United Mine Workers, represented by John L. Lewis, who was chairman of the committee; Amalgamated Clothing Workers; International Ladies' Garment Workers' Union; United Textile Workers; International Union of Mine, Mill and Smelter Workers; and International Association of Oil Field, Gas Well and Refinery Workers. Two union presidents, Charles P. Howard of the International Typographical Union, who became secretary of the committee, and Max Zaritsky of the United Hatters, Cap and Millinery Workers, participated as individuals without committing their organizations to the movement. The following four unions joined shortly after the formation of the committee: International Union of United Automobile Workers; United Rubber Workers; Amalgamated Association of Iron, Steel and Tin Workers; and Federation of Flat Glass Workers.

some 32 other groups or "organizing committees" established to recruit workers in various industries.

John L. Lewis, president of the United Mine Workers, was elected to lead the CIO. The constitutional structure of the new organization resembled that of the AFL. It provided basically for a loose federation of autonomous national unions governed by an executive board composed of a representative from each affiliated union, a board of nine vice presidents, a secretary-treasurer, and a president, all elected at annual conventions of delegates from affiliated unions.

The difficulties between the AFL and CIO did not prevent the growth of unionism. On the contrary, the rivalry generated by the two large federations stimulated the organizing efforts of the unions in each group. By the end of 1941, union membership had climbed to between 10 and 11 million. This was more than double the membership at the time the Committee for Industrial Organization began its campaigns in the large steel, automobile, and textile industries.

During the first flush of this new growth, enthusiasm and emotions ran at a high pitch. As workers poured into unions, many employers were overwhelmed by the ground swell. When companies resisted, strikes frequently occurred. New tactics were used. Some unions demonstrated their militancy by staging "sitdown" strikes during which striking workers stayed inside the plant but refused to work or permit strikebreakers to enter the buildings. Sitdown strikes, for a short period, dramatized the attempts of auto and rubber workers to organize several large companies. Some employers, on the other hand, sought to use strikebreakers or "scabs" to replace their union employees and stored guns, tear gas, and other weapons in their plants for ready use in combating strikes or organizing efforts. These actions provoked occasional outbursts of violence but seldom on the scale that had been experienced during the formative period of unionism before World War I. As the newer unions gained maturity and employers recognized them as representatives of their workers, relations between labor and management gradually improved. More and more workers were protected by written agreements setting forth their wages, hours, and working conditions.

Despite these gains, which were real and substantial, the number of strikes remained relatively high. In 1941, as prices moved upward and production and profits rose, stimulated by the war in Europe, stoppages became more frequent. A few of these controversies were provoked by Communist sympathizers who, before Hitler's attack on Russia in June 1941, favored an "isolationist" policy for American aid to Europe. (After the German invasion of the Soviet Union they became full-fledged "interventionists.") Most of the prewar labor-management conflicts, however, revolved around demands for better wages and greater union security.

CHAPTER IV

THE SECOND WORLD WAR AND RECONVERSION

The attack on Pearl Harbor brought labor and management together in a common cause. Three years later, the war's end signaled the beginning of a new round of battles between the unions and employers. During reconversion, management said unreasonable wage demands were being made of them; labor unions complained that Federal legislation, newly enacted, would effectively cripple them.

The War Years, 1942–45

Shortly after the declaration of war on December 8, 1941, President Roosevelt called a conference of union and industry leaders. At the conclusion of the meetings, the President announced a voluntary pledge from union leaders not to sanction strikes for the duration of the war in return for a pledge by management representatives not to sanction lockouts. These pledges were parts of an agreement leading to establishment of a National War Labor Board to consider all labor-management disputes affecting the war effort, and to provide procedures for their peaceful settlement. This Board, set up in January 1942, was composed of representatives from labor, management, and the general public. Regional boards were organized on a similar basis to handle local controversies. As in the earlier National Defense Mediation Board, which functioned from March to November 1941 to adjust disputes affecting the rearmament program, labor representation was equally divided between the AFL and CIO. By October 1942, it had become necessary to put into effect widespread controls over prices and wages, and the

War Labor Board also became the agency for the stabilization of wages.

In December 1942, representatives from three major labor groups (AFL, CIO, and Railway Brotherhoods) were appointed to the Management-Labor Policy Committee, a consulting body for the War Manpower Commission. Similar joint committees were appointed in the regions and local areas to assist in the overall program of providing workers for war industries. These committees gave practical advice and suggestions in the training, recruitment, and transfer of workers.

Organized labor also played an active role in many phases of the Government's war production program. It was represented on the first defense agency—the Advisory Commission to the Council of National Defense, established in May 1940. With the creation of the Office of Production Management (OPM) in January 1941, Sidney Hillman, president of the Amalgamated Clothing Workers of America (CIO), was appointed by President Roosevelt to share authority

Two GI's watch construction of Philadelphia's USO-Labor Plaza during World War II. AFL and CIO unions donated their labor to the project.

with the Director General of OPM, William S. Knudsen, president of the General Motors Corp.

Under the auspices of the War Production Board, a successor agency to the OPM, labor-management committees were established in many plants to stimulate output and reduce absenteeism. In addition, most of the other war agencies established plans whereby the unions participated in various Federal programs.

With the marked rise in employment, and wider union recognition, union membership increased. Assurance that unions would not be undermined by foregoing their right to strike or by wartime shifts in employment found expression in the War Labor Board's "maintenance-of-membership" formula applied in a number of key situations. In lieu of the closed or union shop sought by unions, this provided in general that workers need not join the union to retain employment, but once choosing to become members must maintain membership for the duration of the agreement. During the war, union membership steadily increased at the rate of about a million workers a year; the greatest gains were in the steel, shipbuilding, aircraft, automotive, and other war industries. Between 1941 and 1945, many unions in the metal trades doubled and tripled their membership. The United Automobile Workers (CIO) in 1945 reported a total dues-paying membership of 1,052,000, the largest recorded by an American union up to that time.

Wage increases were largely held in check by the Government's stabilization policy, as exemplified by the War Labor Board's "Little Steel" formula which sought to confine general increases in wage rates to not more than 15 percent above the level on January 1, 1941. Although wages were controlled, workers obtained various so-called "fringe benefits," such as paid vacations and holidays, shift differentials, and insurance and pension plans.

Collective bargaining agreements were negotiated or extended over large sections of industry during the war. Strikes occurred, but union leaders and Government representatives sought their speedy settlement. Some issues were postponed when it was found that they could not be settled within the existing framework of controls; thus pressures were built up which erupted after the war.

Extension of union membership to workers without regard to race, creed, or nationality, which had been gradually gaining support, was accelerated during the war. Expanded employment of Negroes, particularly in the mass-production industries, necessitated their acceptance into the unions on an equal basis if standards of wages and working conditions were to be maintained. In many unions, prejudices which had existed through the years gradually broke down as white and Negro workers learned to respect each other as fellow workers on the job. Some unions which had previously refused to admit Negroes to membership' relaxed their rules and removed racial restrictions from their constitutions. The Federal Government's Fair Employment Practices Committee aided in eliminating some of the more severe instances of discrimination in industry.

Labor-Management Relations, 1945–47

The end of hostilities in 1945 confronted organized labor and employers with a host of new problems. More than 10 million service men and women were demobilized in the 12 months following V–J Day, August 14, 1945. Thousands of factories retooled to meet the demands of a civilian, peacetime economy.

Many factories cut their scheduled hours from wartime levels of 48 or more a week to the prewar level of 40. Some shut down temporarily or permanently. Wage earners, confronted with losses in "take-home" pay, sought to maintain their wartime earnings which had included substantial overtime pay at premium rates. Union demands soon crystallized

into requests for wage-rate increases of about 30 percent—
the approximate advance the workers deemed necessary to
preserve their former weekly earnings. Many employers,
uncertain of the speed with which reconversion could be
accomplished and opposed to the continuation of price and
other wartime controls, voiced their inability to meet these
wage proposals.

This conflict between labor and management was further
aggravated by the partial termination of stabilization restraints which had held the upward movement of the cost
of living and of rates of pay within moderate bounds during
the war years. Both labor and management wanted to bargain, free of these restrictions. These desires were expressed
by many representatives of labor and of management as the
war neared an end and were reflected in Government policy
as hostilities ceased. On August 16, 1945—less than 48
hours after V–J Day—President Harry S. Truman announced that the National War Labor Board would be
terminated by the end of the year. During the war, the
Board had weathered numerous crises, but pressure for revision of its "Little Steel" formula, or for outright abandon-
ment of stabilization controls over wages, rose steadily in
1945. On August 18, the President issued an order permitting wage increases without specific Government approval, provided the increases would not serve as a basis for
higher prices or added cost to Federal agencies purchasing
goods or services from contractors. Although a successor
agency to the National War Labor Board was established to
carry on the wage stabilization function, conditions in the
postwar period were such that the efforts of the new National
Wage Stabilization Board had limited effectiveness. The
Board went out of existence in early 1947.

Beginning in the autumn of 1945, a number of strikes
occurred in the oil, automobile, steel, and coal industries.
The widespread unrest prompted President Truman to call
a national labor-management conference in November 1945,

with the hope that some formula for industrial peace could be reached. The conference produced few tangible results, and controversies continued. Altogether, 42 large strikes, each involving 10,000 or more workers, occurred between V–J Day and July 1946.

Out of these disputes, a wage increase "pattern" of 18½ cents an hour evolved for some major mass-production industries, particularly those producing automobiles, steel, electrical equipment, and rubber tires. In resisting postwar wage increases, many employers pointed to the difficulties of absorbing such increases as long as prices of their products remained subject to Government control. Partly as a result of these protests, the Office of Price Administration (OPA), which had "policed" prices during the war, was permitted to expire on June 30, 1946. Although the OPA was revived a month later on a limited basis, by the end of the year virtually all price controls were ended.

The "second round" of postwar renewal of union contracts began in the autumn of 1946. Production by that time had reached record peace-time levels and business was generally prosperous. For the most part, management and labor came to terms without the costly stoppages which had marked the preceding year's bargaining. Workers in the heavy mass-production industries obtained in many instances "package" increases estimated to be worth 15 cents an hour, including the value of added holidays with pay, health and welfare provisions, or other "fringe benefits."

New Labor Legislation: The Taft–Hartley Act

There were many causes of industrial unrest and work stoppages in 1945 and 1946. Collective bargaining was still comparatively new in many situations; a considerable measure of employer opposition to unions existed; some unions, recently formed or growing rapidly, could not maintain

union discipline under the accumulation of wartime grievances, or accustom themselves to the less militant methods
of collective bargaining after winning recognition. Neither
group adjustment nor individual self-discipline was aided by
the wholesale shifting of workers to war industries and new
industrial centers and then to other jobs and locations during
reconversion. The quick withdrawal of wartime public controls over labor-management relations and also over production, prices, and wages placed additional responsibilities
upon both unions and employers at a time when the cost of
living was rising rapidly.

The series of postwar work stoppages symbolized serious
industrial unrest in the public mind. Strike idleness as a
percentage of total working time (perhaps the best measure
for comparison over a period of years) began to rise soon
after the war from the unusually low wartime levels. Even
in 1937, a prewar year of above average strike activity,
strike idleness had been less than 0.5 percent of total working time; in 1946, it was 1.43 percent—the highest ever
recorded.

The unsettled labor-management situation after the war
revived and greatly strengthened opposition to the Wagner
Act. Senator Robert A. Taft, a leader in the demand for
change, argued that although the act had been passed to aid
unions in maintaining an appropriate "balance" of rights
and responsibilities between workers and employers, it had
gone "far beyond" such a balance in its actual administration. He and Congressman Fred A. Hartley sponsored a re-
writing of the act. The resulting measure, the Labor Management Relations (Taft-Hartley) Act, 1947, gained such
widespread support that despite strong objections by organized labor and a Presidential veto, it became law on June
23, 1947.

Some provisions of collective agreements which many
unions had obtained or sought were banned or limited under
the revised law. Provision for the so-called "closed shop"

can no longer be included in agreements. Other widely adopted provisions of agreements, such as the union shop, checkoff of union dues, welfare funds, and contract termination arrangements, are regulated.

The concept of striking a "balance" between unions and employers led to the inclusion of a list of "unfair labor practices" applying to unions, along with the list applying to employers. Among various other practices, refusal to bargain in good faith, engaging in secondary boycotts, stopping work over a jurisdictional or interunion dispute, and charging excessive initiation fees to keep new members out of a union are considered by the law to be unfair. Employers, as well as workers, are permitted to appeal to the National Labor Relations Board against unions in connection with such practices. Certain practices may be penalized by court action and law suits for damages. Restrictions on the use of injunctions are eased. One section (14b) of the act allows the States to adopt more restrictive legislation against union security clauses than is provided in the Federal law.

Special rules were written into the Taft-Hartley Act for handling controversies or strikes which, in the judgment of the President, create or threaten emergencies by imperiling the national health or safety. In any such dispute or strike, the President is authorized to appoint a "board of inquiry" to investigate the facts. Thereafter, a court injunction can be obtained forbidding the occurrence or continuance of a stoppage for a period of 80 days. During that "cooling off" or "waiting" period, further efforts are to be made to settle the dispute. If no voluntary agreement can be arranged within 60 days, the employees are to be polled by secret ballot as to whether they will accept the "final offer" of the employer. After all these steps are taken, however, the injunction must be dissolved whether or not the dispute is settled. By the end of 1969 this procedure had been used 29 times.

The Taft-Hartley Act also removed the Federal Mediation and Conciliation Service from the Department of Labor and established it as a separate agency of the Government. This Service offers assistance to labor and management in arriving at peaceful settlement of labor disputes, particularly if they threaten substantial interruption of interstate commerce. Possessing no law enforcement authority, the Service operates through mediators who rely wholly on the persuasive techniques of mediation and conciliation to perform their duties.

Federal law does not prohibit workers from striking, except for employees of the Federal Government. Some State and local governments restrict the right of public employees as well as employees of certain public utilities to strike.

Union opposition to the Taft-Hartley Act was intense in the first few years after its passage. The act was denounced as a "slave labor" law and its repeal became a major goal of the labor movement. Many proposals were made for changes in the new law by its critics and also by its sponsors —changes which, for the most part, would ease the restrictions on unions. Revision proved to be difficult, partly because of the problem of reconciling the views of those who were fearful of going too far in modifying the law with the views of those who felt that any obtainable amendments would not satisfy their objections. By 1951, practical circumstances had brought about general agreement to repeal the requirement that elections be held to validate union-shop agreements. Experience had shown that large majorities of workers in nearly all cases voted for the union shop. Accordingly, the law was amended to eliminate this requirement.

Unions, in the meantime, directed renewed attention to restrictive legislation in the States. Against union opposition, laws in some of the States, particularly in the South, went beyond Taft-Hartley Act restrictions by prohibiting not only closed-shop contracts but also union-shop agreements, maintenance-of-membership agreements, or related forms of union security. This State action was permissible under section 14 (b) of the Taft-Hartley Act. Measures of this type were described by proponents as "right to work" laws; union officials called them "right to wreck" laws. In 1969, these laws were in effect in 19 States, not including Louisiana which repealed its law in 1956 but retained union security restrictions for agricultural laborers and certain farm processing workers.

The Taft-Hartley Act was again amended, through the Labor-Management Reporting and Disclosure Act of 1959, which is described in chapter V.

CHAPTER V

CHANGES IN THE LABOR MOVEMENT, 1947-68

For about 10 years after the passage of the Taft–Hartley Act in 1947, trade union membership expanded at about the same rate as nonagricultural employment was increasing. At the same time, an aggressive collective bargaining approach opened up new vistas for American workers. (See next chapter.) The Korean emergency brought labor leaders again into prominence. The prestige of the labor movement seemed at its highest when the AFL and CIO merged in December 1955, after 20 years of often bitter and costly rivalry. Public fear of Communist domination of unions had been allayed before the merger, and the new Federation set its sights on other vexing problems. Yet, in the years following the merger, the largest union in the Federation (Teamsters) was expelled; the Labor-Management Reporting and Disclosure (Landrum–Griffin Act) brought the Government directly into the regulation of union affairs on a broad scale; union membership began to decline, both in absolute and relative numbers for the first time since the depression; a host of writers began to discuss what they felt was a growing crisis in American labor; and the Auto Worker (UAW), another of the larger AFL–CIO unions, began to attack the AFL–CIO leadership. This union left the AFL–CIO in July 1968 and with the Teamsters, formed the Alliance for Labor Action. Two decades of successes and setbacks for the labor movement had passed.

AFL and CIO Clean House

In the postwar reappraisal of the labor movement, charges of Communist or corrupt influences in union ranks were thrown at the CIO and AFL, and the two Federations were compelled by pressures from within and without to deal forcefully with disruptive elements. Their actions on these issues diminished one of the obstacles to merger.

Unions often have advocated political and social change, but, with minor exceptions, by "due process" in the sense of dependence on legal, constitutional, and democratic methods. Communists, therefore, in their efforts to make use of unions, usually disguised their own real motives. Organized Communist activity in the labor movement began in 1920, when the Trade Union Education League (TUEL) was founded. The TUEL at first rejected dual or competing unionism and adopted a policy of "boring from within" the established unions. Its efforts failed. The Trade Union Unity League, formed in 1928 as the successor to the TUEL, for a time

Sound trucks are used for a register-and-vote rally in Brooklyn, N.Y., sponsored by COPE.

gave up the idea of "boring from within" and undertook to organize industrial unions outside of the AFL. That effort to split the labor movement failed.

After the CIO was formed, the Communists shifted their attention mainly to that organization because its rapid growth provided opportunities for infiltration. Some Communists became organizers and union officials. However, they were less interested in union activities than in support of the "party line." Their espousal of Soviet Russia became increasingly obvious and at the same time increasingly distasteful to CIO leaders and members.

In 1949 and 1950, 11 unions charged with Communist domination were expelled from the CIO. The majority of the members of the expelled unions were not in sympathy with their leaders, however, and in the following years formed or joined other unions affiliated with the AFL or the CIO. As a noteworthy instance, the International Union of Electrical, Radio, and Machine Workers was chartered as a CIO union to replace the ousted United Electrical, Radio and Machine Workers. Only 2 of the 11 unions forced out of the CIO still survived as unaffiliated unions in 1969— the United Electrical Workers and the Longshoremen's and Warehousemen's Union.[3] The combined membership of the ousted unions, including membership outside the continental United States, has dropped by two-thirds from around 875,000 at the time of expulsion.

The AFL was not involved with communism among the officers of its affiliated national unions. The Federation, how-

---

[3] The other nine unions expelled by the CIO were the Fur and Leather Workers; the Office and Professional Workers; the Food, Tobacco, Agricultural, and Allied Workers; the United Farm Equipment and Metal Workers; the Fishermen and Allied Workers; the Public Workers; the Marine Cooks and Stewards; the Mine, Mill and Smelter Workers; and the American Communications Association. All of these unions have merged with other unions or have disbanded.

ever, had to contend with another kind of problem. The International Longshoremen's Association (ILA), a long-time affiliate, was accused by the New York State Crime Commission of corruption, racketeering, and other objectionable practices affecting operation of the Port of New York. Efforts by the Executive Council of the AFL to get the union to clean up its affairs were unsuccessful and, in an unprecedented action, expulsion of the union, by the Federation convention, followed in 1953. A new union was chartered by the AFL, but it failed to dislodge the old ILA. After a bitter contest on the docks and in the courts, the ILA was certified by the National Labor Relations Board as the collective bargaining representative for the New York area dock workers. In 1959, the ILA was readmitted (on a 2-year probationary basis) to the merged AFL–CIO after satisfying the Executive Council that it had cleaned house. The ILA affair, however, was just the beginning of an involved series of developments which ultimately, through the enactment of the Labor-Management Reporting and Disclosure (Landrum-Griffin) Act of 1959, brought the Federal Government more directly into union practices.

Steps Toward Merger

The drive for amalgamation of the two Federations, thwarted many times since 1935 by unyielding attitudes and problems, was set on course 3 years—almost to the day—before its fulfillment. On November 25, 1952, George Meany was elected president of the AFL by the Executive Council to succeed the late William Green. On the same day, the Council took unanimous action to reactivate a committee authorized to seek the road to unity with the CIO. Less than 2 weeks later, the 14th CIO convention elected Walter P. Reuther to the presidency vacated by the death of Philip Murray and likewise authorized its officers to explore the path of unity. Past failures, notably the dissolution in August

Samuel Gompers

William Green

John L. Lewis

Philip Murray

George Meany   Walter P. Reuther

Four Secretaries of Labor meet to celebrate 50th anniversary of Department of Labor, March 1963. (Frances Perkins, James P. Mitchell, Arthur J. Goldberg, W. Willard Wirtz.)

AFL Executive Council in 1909: front—John B. Lennon, Tailors; James Duncan, Granite Cutters; President Samuel Gompers; John Mitchell, Mine Workers; Secretary-Treasurer Frank Morrison; rear—Denis A. Hayes, Glass Bottle Blowers; John R. Alpine, Plumbers; William D. Huber, Carpenters; James O'Connell, Machinists; Max Morris, Clerks; and Joseph F. Valentine, Molders.

A union-management collective bargaining session.

Union members learn the principles and techniques of time and motion study at a training class.

Union summer school sessions are an important part of worker training.

1951 of the United Labor Policy Committee, formed by the AFL and CIO, and railroad unions in December 1950 during the Korean hostilities to present labor's views to the Government on national problems, were submerged in the hope that the new leadership would be able to make a fresh start.

The foundation for unity was laid with the negotiation of the no-raiding agreement in June 1953 and its approval by

Walter P. Reuther and George Meany celebrate the historic merger of the AFL–CIO in 1955.

both federation conventions in the fall of that year. This agreement declared that a union affiliated with one organization would not try to recruit members and organize a plant or shop where bargaining relations already existed with an affiliate of the other organization. It became effective on June 9, 1954, for the 65 AFL and 29 CIO affiliates which, up to that time, had approved its terms. The 1954 AFL and CIO conventions hailed this accomplishment as a constructive step in ending wasteful interunion jurisdictional conflicts and set their sights for the creation of a single trade union organization through the process of merger.

The "Agreement for the Merger," setting forth the procedure by which merger would be effected and establishing the framework for a new constitution, was adopted by a Joint Unity Committee composed of key AFL and CIO leaders, on February 9, 1955. It was ratified by the executive groups of the two Federations shortly thereafter. The drafting of the proposed constitution continued through 1955; the final version was approved by the AFL's Executive Council and the CIO's Executive Board on the eve of the final conventions of each of the Federations. The problem of naming the merged Federations so that both participants would feel equally honored was resolved in midyear in the tradition associated with newspaper mergers, namely, the continuation of both official names.

Merger Achieved

A new era in American labor history opened on December 5, 1955, in New York City with the formation of the American Federation of Labor and Congress of Industrial Organizations—the AFL–CIO. The merger of the two Federations, rivals since 1935, brought into one organization unions representing approximately 16 million workers, including Canadian members, or between 85 and 90 percent of the membership claimed by all unions in the United States.

The first convention of the AFL–CIO adopted a constitution, elected officers, and conducted its carefully planned business with a unanimity which was openly recognized as an expression of unity rather than as an indication that all disputes were settled and all problems solved. The merger was a combination of top structures and a reconciliation of broad outlook and policies. Consolidation of unity down the line, as all the delegates knew, was yet to come. Optimism that this too could be accomplished appeared high on this eventful occasion.

The December 1955 founding convention of the AFL–CIO established a policy and administrative structure generally

Headquarters building of the AFL–CIO in Washington, D.C.

similar to that which existed in the two former Federations. The convention of delegates representing the affiliated unions continued to be the policy formulating body. Conventions, however, were scheduled at 2-year intervals, instead of annually. The governing body between conventions was an Executive Council composed of the president, secretary-treasurer, and 27 vice presidents. A small official body—an Executive Committee—was created to "advise and consult with the president and the secretary-treasurer." The Executive Committee, composed of six vice presidents (initially three from the AFL and three from the CIO) was scheduled to meet bimonthly but was abolished at the 1967 AFL–CIO convention. Finally, a General Board, consisting of the 29 members of the Executive Council and a principal officer of each of the affiliated unions and departments, was created. This larger group met at the call of the president. Its function was to consider policy matters referred to it by the Executive Council and the Executive Officers.

George Meany, former AFL president, and William F. Schnitzler, former AFL secretary-treasurer, were elected president and secretary-treasurer, respectively, of the new Federation. Lane Kirkland replaced Schnitzler as secretary-treasurer in 1969. Walter P. Reuther, former CIO president, became head of a newly created Industrial Union Department and a vice president of the AFL–CIO. When Reuther's union left the AFL–CIO in 1968, I. W. Abel, president of the Steelworkers Union, became head of the Industrial Union Department.

Structurally, other changes also occurred. The Industrial Union Department was formed to promote the interests and deal with the problems of unions having membership organized on an industrial basis. This department took its place alongside the existing former AFL departments—building and construction trades, metal trades, union label and service trades, maritime trades, and railroad employees. In addition, a Department of Organization was established to coordinate drives for union membership. In 1967, a Council of Scientific, Professional, and Cultural Employees was set up to coordinate union activity among this growing part of the labor force. In addition, various standing committees, such as those on civil rights, community services, and ethical practices, now had members from both the AFL and CIO on them. When the merger took place, staff departments in the AFL and CIO, such as those for political education, international affairs, publicity, economic research, education, and others, were consolidated. Former State and local bodies of the two Federations were required to merge within 2 years, but in many cases a longer period was necessary.

For the merger of international union affiliates of the new Federation, the constitution encouraged but did not require such amalgamations. Existing concepts of "autonomy" were preserved. Conflicts between unions competing in the same industry, craft, or area were to be adjusted voluntarily, with the assistance of the president and the Executive Council. The no-raiding agreement and the AFL and CIO arrangements for resolving internal disputes among former affiliates were continued for all those unions which had signed separate pacts.

The Federation's constitution took a strong stand against "Communists, Fascists, and other totalitarians" and denied affiliation to any union "officered, controlled, or dominated" by them. Workers were to share equally in the full benefits of union organization "without regard to race, color, creed, national origin, or ancestry." The Federation further promised to protect the labor movement from corrupt influences. The constitution provided for a Committee on Ethical Practices, to assist the Executive Council in keeping the Federation free from any taint of corruption or communism. This committee was empowered to recommend suspension or expulsion of any union in which undesirable influences gained control.

As part of its function, the committee in 1956 and 1957 drafted six codes which were approved by the AFL–CIO Executive Committee. Designed to guide member unions in the conduct of union affairs, these codes related to local union charters; health and welfare funds; racketeers, crooks, Communists and Fascists; conflicts of interest in the investments and business activities of union officials; financial practices of unions; and union democratic processes. The codes were formally approved by the 1957 convention.

Continuing Problems

Despite the high hopes, optimism, and public good will attending the merger, subsequent years found the AFL–CIO deep in vexing internal problems and increasingly on the defensive on several fronts. Old problems—corruption and irregularities among union officials, jurisdictional conflicts, and charges of racial discrimination—remained. Although substantial progress later was made toward their solution, many persons within and without the labor movement continued dissatisfied with the AFL–CIO's program, particularly in the area of racial discrimination. During the latter part of the 1950's and early 1960's, the public became more interested in the problems of increasing unemployment, and beginning in 1966, growing inflation; the effects of rapidly advancing technology on the organized and organizable sectors of the labor force; the inability of the Federation to put into effect the organizing pledges of the merger; and the AFL–CIO's positions on foreign policy. The charge that the AFL–CIO was failing to meet these problems, old and new, resulted in increasing criticism of the organization from those outside the labor movement.

The concern of the AFL–CIO with unethical and corrupt practices was greatly heightened by revelations flowing out of the work of two Senate committees, first the Senate Subcommittee on Welfare and Pension Plans in 1954–56 and later the Senate Select Committee on Improper Activities in the Labor or Management Field, which held hearings in 1957–59. The AFL–CIO moved quickly against offending affiliates. During 1956 and 1957, six unions were brought before the Ethical Practices Committee and, after hearings, were ordered by the Executive Council to purge themselves of corrupt influences. Subsequently, the December 1957 convention of the AFL–CIO expelled the Teamsters, Bakery Workers, and Laundry Workers, with a combined membership of approximately 1.6 million, for failing to accept and carry through the recommendations of the Executive Council. The Distillery Workers remained on probation, and the United Textile Workers was restored to good standing. The Allied Industrial Workers, by the time of the convention, had complied with Executive Council orders.

Immediately after the expulsion of the Bakery Workers, a new charter was issued to dissident locals of this union to form the American Bakery and Confectionery Workers' International Union (the two unions merged in late 1969). Similarly, the jurisdiction formerly held by the Laundry Workers was assigned to the Laundry and Dry Cleaning International Union. However, no new union was chartered to compete with the International Brotherhood of Teamsters, which continued as an unaffiliated union.

Although AFL–CIO leaders attempted to deal with corrupt elements within the Federation to the extent of their authority, pressures for legislative remedies built up as the congressional hearings progressed. In August 1958, the Congress passed the Welfare and Pension Plans Disclosure Act, and in September 1959, the Labor-Management Reporting and Disclosure Act. The latter act marked a significant turning point in the involvement of the Federal Government in internal union affairs.

Protection of the large and rapidly growing funds and the money handled in the administration of welfare and pension plans received the first attention from Congress. The Welfare and Pension Plans Disclosure Act was originally a simple disclosure statute, rather than a regulatory measure, which required administrators of all health, insurance, pen-

sion, and supplementary unemployment compensation plans
covering more than 25 workers to file descriptions of their
plans and annual financial reports with the U.S. Secretary
of Labor. (Union officials administer or participate in the
administration of only a small proportion of the plans covered by the act.) These reports were to be made available
to plan participants, and were also to be open to public
inspection. In passing this law, Congress believed that the
responsibility and accountability of management and union
officials might be improved by making these records available for examination. Experience with the law in actual
operation demonstrated that it was relatively ineffective in
carrying out these aims. In 1962, with the support of the
AFL–CIO, the law was amended and strengthened mate-
rially, with the new rules for reporting, bonding of fund
officials, and penalties for its violation, both as to reporting
and the conduct of fund affairs. Reporting requirements for
small plans were eased.

The Labor-Management Reporting and Disclosure (Landrum-Griffin) Act had much greater implications for the
labor movement. This far-reaching act was based upon findings by Congress of a need "to eliminate or prevent improper
practices on the part of labor organizations, employers,
labor relations consultants, and their officers and representatives which distort and defeat the policies of the Labor
Management Relations Act, 1947, as amended, and the
Railway Labor Act, as amended." The act contains seven
titles. Title I is called the Bill of Rights of Members of
Labor Organizations, and is designed to protect certain
rights of individuals in relations with their union. These
rights generally relate to participation in union affairs; protection from unwarranted financial burdens; and the right
to testify, to be informed of union agreements, and of fair
hearing in disciplinary actions. The rights under this title
can be enforced by suits in Federal district courts.

Titles II through VI deal with reporting by labor organizations and their officers and employees, and by employers

and their labor relations consultants; prevention of abuses in union trusteeship; standards for union elections; and safeguards for labor organizations, among other matters. Severe penalties are provided for violation of several of these provisions. Title VII amends the Labor Management Relations Act, 1947, to eliminate the "no-man's land" in Federal-State jurisdictions, permit voting by economic strikers, control secondary boycotts, limit hot-cargo agreements, and regulate organizational and recognition picketing. The act also eliminates the requirement for non-Communist affidavits from union officials.

The problem of jurisdictional disputes, particularly as related to organization and representation claims of competing unions, carried over from before the merger and was aggravated thereafter by declining job opportunities. An attempt to deal with the issue was made at the 1959 AFL–CIO convention, but a plan of action foundered on disagreement between the Industrial Union Department and the Building and Construction Trades Department. A peace formula, supported by all but one of the affiliates was agreed upon at the 1961 convention. It provided for a system of mediation and arbitration, and was supported by sanctions to be imposed by the Executive Council. The plan reportedly has had a high degree of success. Yet, jurisdictional problems remain—for example, in organizing white-collar employees. A dispute has continued over who should represent clerks working in industrial firms—the Office and Professional Employees Union which has jurisdiction over white-collar employees, or an industrial union which has jurisdiction over workers in a given industry.

Just a year before the merger of the AFL and the CIO, the Supreme Court ordered the end of segregation in schools. This decision marked the beginning of a major movement to integrate the black citizen into American society. Part of the movement involved criticisms of the AFL–CIO. Some labor leaders within the AFL–CIO, led by A. Philip Ran-

Trend in Union Membership

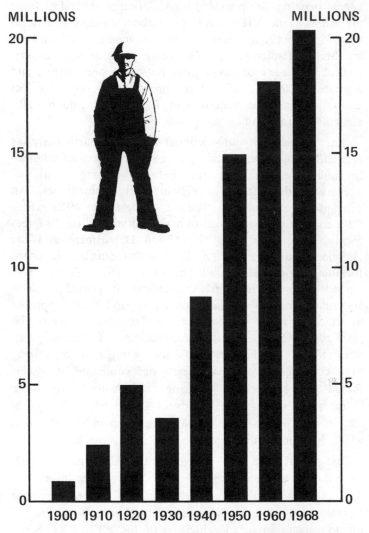

MILLIONS   MILLIONS

20   20

15   15

10   10

5   5

0   0

1900 1910 1920 1930 1940 1950 1960 1968

BASED ON
UNION REPORTS

dolph, then president of the Brotherhood of Sleeping Car Porters, criticized the Federation for at best doing very little to help the Negro worker, and at worst, for discriminating against him. This criticism was echoed outside organized labor by organizations such as the National Association for the Advancement of Colored People. These critics argued that the AFL–CIO had not acted on its own initiative to end discrimination; that much of what had been done involved good intentions but little action; and that even the good intentions were mainly felt at the top of the labor movement, not at the local union level. Although the AFL–CIO had taken firm action against Communism and corruption within labor, it was charged that it had not acted as firmly against discrimination. Particularly in the construction industry, the unions had actively discriminated against Negroes—for example, in making entrance to apprenticeship programs difficult.

The AFL–CIO answered these attacks by taking various actions: at convention after convention, it reaffirmed its traditional opposition to all forms of discrimination based on race, creed, color, or national origin. Compliance machinery within the AFL–CIO was strengthened although expulsion of unions which continued to discriminate was rejected. It argued that the way to solve the problem was to keep the recalcitrant union within labor's house. In supporting civil rights and anti-poverty legislation, the AFL–CIO increasingly broadened its emphasis on the wider scope of the civil rights issues in the community and the country at large. Steps were taken to facilitate preapprenticeship training programs for the disadvantaged, to encourage black citizens to sign up for apprenticeship programs, and to encourage unions to take in such potential apprentices. It helped bring about the situation in which no national union any longer has a Caucasian-only clause in its constitution although some locals continue segregated. The AFL–CIO supported those unions and managements which signed into agreements anti-discrimination clauses. Dissatisfaction with the AFL–CIO continues among civil rights activists who, at times, take their dissatisfactions to the streets and picket the sites where union men are working, particularly in construction, as the blacks demand their share of jobs.

A little more than a decade after the merger, the AFL–CIO's organizing promise remained largely unfulfilled. On the contrary, union membership as a percent of employees in nonagricultural establishments had dropped from 33.4 percent in 1956 to 27.8 percent in 1968. However, absolute membership, after declining every year between 1956 and 1961, began to increase slowly again so that in 1968 unions had about 1.4 million more members than they had in 1956. The forces at work making organizing more difficult or reducing the number of union members included: (1) The changing composition of the labor force, that is, the increasing number and proportion of white-collar workers who have been historically difficult for American unions to organize, and the relative decline in the number of manual or blue-collar workers; (2) the nation's unorganized workers are those most difficult to organize. They include white-collar employees, labor in the South, the Negro, workers in small firms, women and part-time employees and farm labor; (3) the effect of technological change on existing centers of organization, particularly the mass-production industries; (4) the growing sophistication of management in dealing with personnel relations, thereby lessening the desire of workers to join unions; and (5) a continuation of organizational rivalries.

To meet some of these problems, the AFL–CIO coordinated a number of unionization campaigns in specific areas, and gave financial assistance and moral support to organizing drives among farmworkers and public employees. Encouraging notes in organizing included the growth of unionization in the public sector. By 1968, government employee unions had increased by more than 1.2 million members compared with 1956, with 700,000 more joining between 1964 and 1968 alone. In 1968, 1,349,000 em-

Labor Union Membership, Selected Years, 1897–1968 [1]
[In thousands]

Year	Total, all unions	American Federation of Labor	Congress of Industrial Organizations [2]	Unaffiliated
1897	440	265		175
1900	791	548		243
1905	1,918	1,494		424
1910	2,116	1,562		554
1915	2,560	1,946		614
1920	5,034	4,079		955
1925	3,566	2,877		689
1930	3,632	2,961		671
1933	2,857	2,127		730
1935	3,728	3,045		683
1940	8,944	4,247	3,625	1,072
1945	14,796	6,931	6,000	1,865
1947	15,414	7,578	6,000	1,836
1953	17,860	10,778	5,252	1,830
1954	17,955	10,929	5,200	1,826
1955	17,749	16,062		1,688
1956	18,477	16,904		1,573
1957	18,431	16,954		1,476
1958	18,081	14,993		3,088
1959	18,169	15,124		3,044
1960	18,117	15,072		3,045
1961	17,328	14,572		2,756
1962	17,630	14,835		2,794
1963	17,586	14,818		2,768
1964	17,976	15,150		2,825
1965	18,519	15,604		2,915
1966	19,181	16,198		2,983
1967	19,712	16,638		3,074
1968	20,258	15,608		4,650

[1] Includes members outside of the United States, primarily in Canada.
[2] Organized in 1938.
[3] Preliminary.
SOURCE: AFL, 1897–1947, *Proceedings* of Conventions; 1953–60, Bureau of Labor Statistics *Directories* of National and International Labor Unions in the United States. CIO, 1940–47, statements at conventions; 1953–60, BLS *Directories*. Unaffiliated unions, 1897–33, *Ebb and Flow in Trade Unionism*, by Leo Wolman, with 1930–33 adjusted to include membership in the Trade Union Unity League; 1935–47, BLS estimates; 1953–60, BLS *Directories*. Figures for 1955–68 reflect the merger of the AFL and CIO into a single federation.

ployees in the Federal Government belonged to unions compared with 900,000 in 1964, while 804,000 State and local government employees were organized in 1968 as compared with 550,000 in 1964. The reasons for this growth were numerous. They included the growing acceptance of unionization in American life; favorable actions, such as President John F. Kennedy's Executive Order 10988 on Employee-

Management Cooperation in the Federal Service issued in January 1962, and similar steps taken by State and local authorities; organizing drives by unions; greater receptivity of reapportioned legislatures to union demands; civil rights movements supporting unions for the disadvantaged public worker; unfavorable conditions for public employees compared with those of employees in the private sector; and the growth of the number of employees working at public jobs.

Large numbers of public employees such as teachers, and some professional employees such as athletes and nurses, joined professional associations which performed many of the functions of unions, including collective bargaining. Among the most important of these associations are the National Education Association, the Major League Baseball Players Association, and the American Nurses Association.

Public unionism, however, provided new problems for union-management relations. Questions continually debated and studied have dealt with the determination of the appropriate bargaining unit; the scope of bargaining; the source of ultimate decisionmaking power in collective bargaining and in personnel relations; grievance and arbitration procedures; and strikes. Procedures proposed to handle collective bargaining impasses received the most publicity when public employees struck and closed down facilities such as schools and welfare departments, and prevented garbage collection. As public employee strikes increased from 15 in 1958 to 254 in 1968 so did the number of signed, peacefully arrived at agreements. By November 1968, for example, nearly 1,200 agreements had been negotiated covering about 1.2 million employees in 33 Federal departments and agencies. In October 1969, Executive Order 10988 was replaced by President Nixon's Executive Order 11491, Labor-Management Relations in the Federal Service, which, among other changes, provides for binding arbitration to settle disputes over new contract terms.

As the pressure from growing unionization among public employees has prompted local, State, and Federal authorities to think about the need for legislation in this field, similarly the pressure for unionization of farm employees is also caus- ing proposals to be made for legislation to be developed which will take into account this relatively new, but growing, group of farm union members. Farm workers, like public employees, have not been covered by the Wagner Act, the Taft-Hartley Act, or the Landrum-Griffin Act, and pressure is increasing for some legislative innovations.

In sum, then, by 1968, 189 national and international unions with headquarters in the United States had approxi- mately 20.2 million members, including about 1.4 million in areas outside the United States, primarily in Canada. One hundred and twenty-six AFL–CIO affiliates, plus directly associated locals, had 15.6 million members, and 63 un- affiliated national unions had 4.6 million members. In addi- tion, approximately 475,000 members were in single-firm or local unaffiliated unions. (See table.)

Union membership in the United States, excluding Canada, constituted 22.9 percent of the country's total labor force in 1968 and 27.8 percent of all employees in nonagricultural establishments.

In recent years, the UAW had become increasingly critical of the way the AFL–CIO handled such problems as organiz- ing the unorganized, unemployment and poverty, civil rights, and foreign policy issues. These differences, plus the person- ality conflict between George Meany and Walter Reuther, contributed to the latest split in the labor movement which resulted in the formation of the Alliance for Labor Action in July 1968. The Alliance's charter members—the two larg- est unions in the country—were the Teamsters who had been expelled from the AFL–CIO in 1957, and the Auto Workers who had disaffiliated in 1968.

Although it is too early to say what direction the Alliance will take, the ALA has promised to push major organizing drives, and to be more concerned with political action, social reform, and civil rights than it claims the AFL–CIO has been. Despite the fact that George Meany had threatened to expel any union which affiliates with the ALA, the International Chemical Workers Union joined the ALA in August 1969—and was promptly expelled by the AFL-CIO in October.

CHAPTER VI

POSTWAR COLLECTIVE BARGAINING

The lifeblood of trade unionism in the United States has always been the representation of members in negotiations with employers. After World War II and the readjustment period, collective bargaining, which in the major mass production industries was still a young institution, had the opportunity to mature. While the controversies and problems described in the previous chapter swirled about the trade union movement and occupied much of the attention of top officials, the national unions and their locals devoted their efforts to seeking "good" contracts, an expansion in the scope of their agreements, and fair administration of agreements in day-to-day work. Innovation followed upon innovation and improvement upon improvement, and a way of life was forged by the American worker and his employer unknown to previous generations in this country. The strike continued to play its traditional role in collective bargaining, but the trend was toward the peaceful resolution of disputes.

The Taft-Hartley Act defined collective bargaining as "the performance of the mutual obligation of the employer and the representative of the employees to meet at reasonable times and confer in good faith with respect to wages, hours, and other terms and conditions of employment, or the negotiation of an agreement, or any question arising thereunder, and the execution of a written contract. . . ." The statement of a legal duty to bargain collectively and the phrase "other terms and conditions of employment" required interpretation, which was one of the primary functions of the National Labor Relations Board. What seemed to be a simple concept in the beginning evolved through the years into a detailed, complex, and changeable legal framework surrounding collective bargaining and internal union administration. In general, however, established collective bargaining relationships adjusted to the legal formalities and continued from year to year with the responsibility for basic decisions regarding wages, hours, and conditions of employment resting with the parties involved rather than with the law.

By 1966, approximately 140,000 collective bargaining contracts were in force in the United States. About 2,000 of these each covered more than 1,000 workers. Most agreements were single employer agreements, negotiated with a local of a national union and covering a single establishment or plant. However, most of the worker coverage of the 2,000 major agreements was accounted for by multiplant and multiemployer agreements; the latter types were concluded with employers combined into associations for bargaining purposes. Thirty-three unions had more than 1,000 agreements each. Moreover, the concentration of agreements among a small number of unions has been growing. The proportion of agreements held by unions having 5,000 or more agreements each climbed from 32 percent in 1962 to 44 percent in 1966.

During postwar years, agreements increased not only in number and coverage, but in breadth and complexity. This reflected the broadening of the scope of collective bargaining and a tendency toward increased contract detail so as to leave as little doubt as possible subject to later disputes over meaning. The relatively simple agreements of the 1930's thus evolved into elaborate contracts, in some cases over 300 pages in length and covered such issues as: (1) Wages and wage administration; (2) benefits supplemental to wages—holidays, vacations, pensions, health and insurance plans, etc.; (3) working conditions, safety, shop rules, and related subjects; (4) work schedules, hours, shifts, overtime provisions; (5) layoff procedures, seniority, promotion, transfers, etc.; and (6) operative provisions, such as grievance and arbitration procedures, definition of bargaining unit, union security, discipline, duration of contract, etc. Since there was no central union policy regarding any of these issues (the Federations were not directly involved in collective bargaining), and since collective bargaining has always been highly decentralized in the United States, although a recent tendency has been to coordinate bargaining with a number of unions sitting down at the same bargaining table with one company, agreements on the whole have continued to reflect substantial differences among U.S. industries in practices and procedures.

General wage increases and the adoption and liberalization of supplementary fringe benefits dominated collective bargaining throughout most of the postwar period. Between 1958 and 1965, the effects of technological change, unemployment, and other related economic forces were strongly stressed in collective bargaining. This emphasis lessened once unemployment began to drop. Some of the highlights of collective bargaining during the postwar years are described in this chapter, but it must be remembered that the complete history of collective bargaining is recorded in the experience of tens of thousands of employers and local unions, millions of workers, and countless communities across the Nation.

Wages

In the midst of a great diversity in practices among unions and employers, certain trends of wage bargaining emerged after the war. The first and second postwar "rounds" of wage increases, already mentioned, were followed by a third "round" in 1948, which also brought widespread increases and a discernible pattern of wage actions. Thereafter, "rounds" of wage increases gave way to greater diversity of wage change among industries and companies, although pattern bargaining has persisted in certain industries such as automobiles and basic steel. During the latest round in 1968, larger gains in wages and benefits were secured in major collective bargaining settlements than in any other past year for which comparable information is available. For example, workers covered by settlements affecting 1000 workers or more in private industry received an average wage adjustment of 7.2 percent compared with 3.1 percent in 1954. The low during the intervening years was 2.8 percent in 1961; except for 1968, the high was 5.6 percent in 1967.

Two innovations which were to have a strong influence upon wage bargaining were incorporated into a particularly noteworthy agreement negotiated in 1948 by the General Motors Corp. and the Auto Workers. This agreement established for the first time definite formulas relating wages to general productivity increases and also to changes in consumer prices. An annual increase of 3 cents an hour (raised in later contracts), called an annual improvement factor, was to be added to the base rate of each wage classification for the duration of the agreement. It assured the worker that his wage rates would increase at the same rate as the Nation's industrial growth. The agreement also provided for automatic cost-of-living wage adjustments every 3 months, based on changes in the Bureau of Labor Statistics Consumer Price Index. This provision protected the worker's standard of living against price rises. These provisions did not spread to other companies until the original contract was renegotiated in 1950. Thereafter, formal wage "escalation" reached a peak in 1958–59, when about 4 million workers under major agreements were covered. The importance of deferred annual wage increases can be seen by the numbers covered. A peak was reached first in 1957 when more than 5 million workers received deferred wage increases. This year was the high point until 1969, when more than 6 million workers were scheduled to receive a deferred wage raise.

The promise of an annual increase was the more profound change; the real significance of this innovation was not reflected solely in the number of agreements that explicitly followed this example (which were many), but by the extent to which the concept of raising wages in line with advancing national productivity spread in wage arbitration, in minimum wage legislation, and in economic thinking and planning. Assured annual increases also provided the basis for the gradual increase in the duration of agreements to 2 or 3 years, or longer, and contributed greatly to the growing stability of labor-management relations.

Although the major concern of unions and employers centered on changes in general wage levels, day-to-day wage administration problems also entered into collective bargaining to a greater extent. Rate structures, wage differentials, allowances, incentive systems, time studies, production standards, job classification, and job evaluation required wider union responsibilities and training for union officials. In a significant achievement, the Steelworkers and the basic steel companies carried through a joint job evaluation program that has been maintained, with necessary modifications, to the present.

Fringe Benefits

The trade union drive for fringe benefits and related practices during postwar years added new dimensions to compensation and in the economic and social status of the wage earner. Under the traditional wage system, the wage earner had been paid for the number of hours he worked or pieces he produced; if he stopped working because of fatigue, need for a vacation, holiday shutdowns, sickness, disability, old age, or death, income from his employer ceased. Under the comprehensive programs of fringe benefits now provided for in most collective bargaining agreements, the wage earner has certain assurances and protection off the job as well as at work. Some practices reflect acceptance of the principle long advocated by unions that, when a worker is unable to work for reasons beyond his control, his income or security must be sustained, for a time at least, to meet family needs. Certain contract provisions recognize rest and recreation as a part of the employment relationship. To an increasing extent, the wage earner is being compensated for lost working time due to personal reasons, such as a death in the family, or for attending to civic duties, as in serving on a jury. If he continues to work for the same company long enough, or otherwise qualifies for a private pension he may earn some degree of financial security for life.

No longer, then, when unions ask for more, are they only asking for wage increases. They are also demanding an increasing number of fringe benefits. Not everyone agrees on the definition of fringes, but those negotiated by unions and management can be placed mainly in three categories:

1. Extra pay for time worked. This provision covers such items as overtime pay; shift differentials; premium pay for Saturday, Sunday, sixth or seventh day of work, holiday work; call-in pay; profit sharing and bonuses.

2. Pay for time not worked. Included are such items as holidays, vacations, military leave, sick-leave pay, personal excused absences (death in family), jury duty, rest periods, wash-up time, lunch periods, severance pay, Christmas bonuses, education and training subsidies, pay for time spent on grievances and negotiations, and supplementary unemployment benefits.

3. Payments for health and security. These benefits include such items as pensions, group life insurance, hospitalization, group accident and health insurance, and medical insurance covering normal medical care plus dental care, eye care, mental health, alcoholism, and allowance for prescriptions.

The first step in the drive for fringe benefits was to bring the new practices into the collective bargaining agreement; thereafter, efforts were directed to broadening the scope and liberalizing the benefits. Provisions for paid vacations for manual workers started to spread during World War II and became almost a universal practice in the next decade. For long-service employees, length of vacations grew from a week to 4 weeks or more. Extended vacation plans providing 3 months off every 5 years for long service workers in the top half of the seniority roster were negotiated in the steel industry in 1963. In addition, the 1968 negotiations resulted in steelworkers in the bottom half of the seniority list becoming eligible every 5 years for an extended vacation of 3 weeks plus his regular vacation. One fifth of each group, therefore, can take an extended vacation each year. Other unions are securing vacation bonuses for their members whereby workers, on vacation, receive extra pay. Paid holidays were introduced into the auto industry in 1947, but did not reach the steel industry until 1952. This practice, too, became standard in agreements, while the number of paid holidays increased.

Pension plans providing a lifetime supplement to Federal Social Security benefits to qualified workers, and health and insurance plans providing life insurance, accident and sickness benefits, and hospital, surgical, medical, and maternity benefits for workers and their dependents, were perhaps the outstanding innovations of the postwar period. The growth of these practices was stimulated by a favorable tax policy which lessened their costs; the lag in benefit levels of the Federal Social Security program behind living costs; the U.S. Supreme Court's affirmation, in 1949, of a National Labor Relations Board ruling on the employer's legal obligation to bargain on pension plans; and the 1949 report of the Steel Industry Factfinding Board which supported the union position that industry has a social and economic obligation to provide social insurance and pensions to workers. The negotiation of pension and insurance plans gathered momentum in 1950. In 1945, only about a half million workers were covered by any type of health and insurance or pension plan under collective bargaining; by 1966, about 16 million were covered by negotiated health and insurance plans and about 14 million by negotiated pension plans. Nine out of 10 nongovernment workers under union contract had a negotiated health and insurance benefit while 3 out of 4 had retirement plan coverage. Increases in pensions being paid have been so marked, according to one BLS 1968 survey, that retirement income, including private pension and social security payments, will approach preretirement income after taxes for long-service employees. Moreover, after Medicare was passed in 1965, changes were made so that more negotiated plans would cover retired workers and would integrate Medicare with the negotiated health insurance plans.

Another significant innovation was the supplementary unemployment benefit plan (SUB) negotiated by the Ford Motor Co. and the Auto Workers in 1955. Similar plans subsequently spread to cover about 2.5 million workers, largely in the auto and steel industries, while about 600,000 more workers are protected by guaranteed annual wage or employment schemes. Although SUB has not spread to new industries, after its initial upsurge, existing SUB programs have been liberalized. Thus, beginning in December 1968, a Ford worker who has 7 years seniority will be entitled to 95 percent of his normal pay for up to a year during layoffs. Some of these plans are related directly to the effects of technological change. For example, in August 1969, a steelworker, who lost earnings as a result of technological changes or for other reasons, would receive a payment from the supplementary unemployment fund, which would bring his income up to 85 percent of his average quarterly income in the previous year.

Although severance or dismissal pay plans developed slowly during postwar years, they began to spread when the concern over layoffs developed in the early 1960's. Provisions covering other practices, such as formal rest periods, reporting pay, funeral leave, shift premium pay, and jury duty pay, also found their way into more collective bargaining agreements. In addition, job training programs, tuition refunds, and increased contributions to apprenticeship programs are being negotiated more frequently.

Some of the benefits new to wage earners had long been available to many salaried workers and executives. The fringe benefit movement, by encompassing the welfare of the wage earner and his dependents, has had profound social implications, and many unions considered these practices not only as a part of worker remuneration but as obligations which society places upon the employer. Workers in other industrialized countries have protections similar to those available to American workers, but nowhere else are these matters left, to such an extent, to the determination of labor and management rather than to law.

Other Bargaining Issues

Among the dozens of other matters that came within the range of collective bargaining during postwar years, a few merit special note.

As previously mentioned, the Taft-Hartley Act banned the closed shop in industries affecting interstate commerce but permitted union shop and maintenance of membership clauses, subject to State "right-to-work" laws. Through collective bargaining, thereafter, the union shop supplanted the closed shop. Union shop provisions appeared in half the agreements in effect in 1950, exclusive of the railroad and airlines industries. Another 20 percent had maintenance of membership clauses. Since 1950, the proportion of agreements without any union security clause has declined to less than 20 percent. About 9 out of 10 agreements in States without "right-to-work" laws have a union security clause, while the union shop supplanted most of the maintenance of membership clauses. Except for the introduction of the agency shop principle, where the nonmember pays a fee to the union, little activity has taken place on this front in recent years other than in the public sector. In 1951, the Railway Labor Act was amended to permit negotiation of union shop agreements.

While change followed upon change in collective bargaining agreements, hours of work and premium rates for overtime were relatively stable elements. The 40-hour week and time and one-half for overtime, which were also embodied in Federal legislation applicable to interstate commerce, became the standards. Some industries not covered by legislation reduced hours to 40 through collective bargaining; in 1949, about a million nonoperating railroad workers had their work-week reduced from 48 to 40 hours without a reduction in take-home pay. Some industries, particularly apparel, construction, and printing, reduced hours below 40, but the 40-hour straight-time workweek prevailed for most workers under collective bargaining. In recent years, the trade union movement has given some attention to the issue of reducing hours of work and increasing overtime penalty rates to combat unemployment, but no significant change, either in collective bargaining or in legislation, had been achieved by the end of 1969. There have been a few exceptions. For example, Local 3 of the Electrical Workers (IBEW) secured a 25-hour week in 1962, while a number of other unions in printing and construction have negotiated reduced workweeks.

Reflecting the labor movement's increased concern with civil rights, the negotiation of antidiscrimination clauses has become prominent in recent years. These clauses, which generally are directed to hiring and on-the-job discrimination remind the parties of their obligations, encourage minority group members to assert their rights, and guide arbitrators in settling grievances. The real effectiveness of these provisions, however, depends on the good faith of the parties.

Certainly one of the great postwar innovations in labor-management relations was the almost complete acceptance of provisions establishing formal grievance procedures and, as the final step in the process, the arbitration of grievance disputes. The achievements of these procedures are beyond measure. A grievance procedure enables a worker or a group of workers, with the help of a union representative, to express a grievance arising out of day-to-day employment and be assured a fair hearing, all the way up the line if necessary. If such a dispute cannot be settled by mutual agreement, final and binding arbitration by an impartial person selected by the parties provides for a peaceful resolution of the issue. Some countries have labor courts for such problems; the strength and versatility of collective bargaining in the United States is reflected in its ability to devise such flexible alternatives to legal procedures.

Strikes

The strike and the threat of strike, or a lockout, continued during the postwar period as integral parts of the collective bargaining process. In the years following World War II, strike activity appeared to have declined generally, but in 1967 and in 1968, it again began to increase. The decline resulted from a combination of several influences: The growing maturity of labor-management relations; the dilution of the antagonisms carried over from pre-World War II organization campaigns; strengthened Federal and State mediation services; and public and Government pressures to avoid or shorten strikes for economic reasons. Pressures for strikes also stemmed from a number of causes: The desire for a greater voice in negotiations has caused workers to reject more agreements reached by management and union representatives; and the growth of antagonisms in newly organized fields, such as government where strikes increased from 42 in 1965 to 254 in 1968.

The period under consideration (1946–68) opened with the year of greatest strike activity in U.S. history; dropped to the lowest peace-time record since the depression in 1961 and 1963, and then ended with strikes on the increase. In 1946, strike idleness constituted 1.43 percent of the estimated total working time, or more than twice as high as any other year on record. On the other hand, from 1960–63, all 4 years of which were relatively low strike years, strike losses, averaging about 18 million man-days a year, amounted to only 0.12 percent of total working time. In 1968, about 49 million man-days were lost because of strikes, amounting to 0.28 percent of total working time. This level of stoppages was the highest recorded since 1953 when more than 5,000 strikes took place; more man-days of idleness occurred in 1968 than any year since 1959 when 69 million such days were lost. The high points of strike activity between 1946 and 1968 were 1949 (0.44 percent), marked by major strikes in the coal and steel industries; 1952 (0.48 percent), also a year of coal and steel strikes; and 1959 (0.50), the year of the 116-day steel strike, the largest strike of all time in the United States as measured by total man-days of idleness. Thousands of stoppages, ranging from 3,333 in 1960 to 5,117 in 1952 occurred in each of the postwar years, but in any 1 year the number of stoppages was but a small percentage of the number of agreements in existence and the number renegotiated.

The favorable strike record in the early 1960's was attributable largely to the lessening frequency and effect of large strikes, signifying, as in the steel industry, that old patterns of conflict in some major situations were breaking up. On the other hand, the persistence of strikes among smaller companies throughout the postwar period and the increase in stoppages during 1967–68, indicated that the strike was not yet obsolete, particularly in a period of inflation, nor was the implied or open threat of strike likely to be displaced from negotiations by another motivating force as long as decentralized collective bargaining in a free society prevailed.

The national emergency machinery provided under the Taft-Hartley Act to investigate disputes threatening to "imperil the national health or safety" was invoked by the President in 29 situations from the time of its enactment in 1947 through 1969. The stevedoring industry was involved seven times; aircraft-aerospace, five times; atomic energy installations, four; the bituminous coal and the maritime industries, three each. Other industries also were involved, including the basic steel industry in 1959. Injunctions were obtained in 25 of the 29 cases, and the time thus gained usually ended or prevented strikes. High Government officials outside the Federal Mediation and Conciliation Service also became involved in similar types of "emergency" dis-

putes which could not be covered by Taft-Hartley procedures, either because of the act's definition of a "national
emergency" dispute or because the formal procedures were
held to be inappropriate to the situation. As the pressures
of international affairs and national economic issues increased during the postwar period, the possibility, and in
some situations the likelihood, of ultimate Government involvement, should a strike develop, became more and more
a fact of life to union and management representatives in
major industries. The bill providing for compulsory arbitration of the complex work rules dispute between major railroads and five operating unions, enacted in August 1963,
marked the deepest penetration of Federal Government authority into collective bargaining in times of peace.

Collective Bargaining in Transition

Toward the end of the 1950's, the economic base upon
which postwar collective bargaining had largely rested was
shaken by several interrelated forces of steadily mounting
effects: Accelerated technological change or automation; an
increase in foreign competition; changes in the work force,
in particular the relative decline in organized manual worker
occupations and the rise of unorganized white-collar worker
occupations, which weakened the trade union structure; a
high rate of unemployment; and a scarcity of jobs for which
displaced workers and workers in vulnerable occupations and
ages were fitted. Some industries felt these pressures more
than others, and in these industries collective bargaining
began what promised to be a long-term readjustment and
transformation.

New techniques for collective bargaining were devised.
"Human relations" committees and other types of joint study
or continuing bargaining committees were established by
companies and unions in many industries, including steel,
autos, meatpacking, rubber, and electrical equipment. Neu-

tral advisers were brought into some groups. Experiments developing out of committee discussions, such as the Kaiser Steel "long-range sharing" plan and the steel industry's extended vacation plan, were widely acclaimed. In some measure, the need to avoid strikes in major industries was the spur to labor and management, but recognition of the complexity of the new problems and of the need for extensive discussions was also an important factor.

Perhaps one indication of the flexibility of collective bargaining was its response to technological change. For a number of years, when the public was concerned about the negative effect which new technology might have upon employment, union and management negotiated many provisions to cushion its effects upon the worker. Some of these provisions include: the requirement of managements to consult wtih unions before the installation of labor-reducing equipment; attrition plans to protect employed workers; the phasing of the installation of new equipment; the organization of special study committees to analyze the implications of such changes; special automation funds to which the employer contributes; various forms of guaranteed employment or guaranteed minimum income; extended seniority units to protect the transfer rights of affected workers; company paid retraining; moving expenses for relocated workers; severance pay; supplementary unemployment benefits; and fewer hours of work through shorter work weeks, more holidays, longer vacations, or earlier retirements.

Throughout the industries and communities most directly affected by the new forces, the realization grew that unions and managements had to use collective bargaining more imaginatively, but that collective bargaining had limitations. Collective bargaining was more effective in helping the employed than the unemployed, low paid workers in some segments of the economy, the underemployed, or the new entrant into the labor market. Consequently, the labor movement, like many groups outside organized labor, moved to the legislative halls to work toward helping these disadvantaged groups. As a result, the AFL–CIO has supported large scale increases in public service employment so that the unemployed could find work; the raising of the statutory minimum wage to at least $2 an hour and the expansion of the groups covered by the minimum; a national job-training program; a nationwide Federal employment service authorized to grant relocation allowances; enforcement of anti-discrimination legislation; improved education for all; low-income housing; increased health-care; comprehensive national health insurance; more day-care centers; better social services; comprehensive and expanded social insurance programs, including old age, survivors and disability insurance, unemployment insurance, and workmen's compensation; and an improved public welfare program.

Although the labor movement continues to be primarily concerned with collective bargaining, it is also concerned with public issues. Moreover, the labor movement no longer only takes positions on public issues which affect its members solely as union members as in the early days of the AFL, but it now supports issues which affect its members as citizens. Just as the labor movement has expanded the meaning of the term "more" in collective bargaining, the labor movement also has widened the scope of the "more" it seeks in the political field.

CHAPTER VII

SOME OUTSTANDING FEATURES OF THE LABOR MOVEMENT

The American labor movement, as it has grown and evolved, has been fashioned by the character, spirit, and aspirations common to the workers of the United States. American unions have rarely expressed either utopian or revolutionary aims. They have usually been animated by the same philosophy that guided Samuel Gompers, leader of the AFL until his death in 1924. Gompers sought to have unions recognized by employers as representatives of their employees; and he constantly tried to convince the public at large that unions should be accepted as "an integral social element" seeking labor's advancement in a manner consistent with general reform and progress and with "a better life for all."

Outlook and Aims

These concepts and aims are likewise emphasized in the AFL–CIO constitution. The first aim set forth is the securing of "improved wages, hours, and working conditions." The Federation should encourage unorganized workers to form "unions of their own choosing." All workers, "without regard to race, creed, color, national origin, or ancestry," should "share equally in the benefits of union organization." Participation in the Nation's political affairs is strongly favored, but unions should not come under the control of any political party. Workers are encouraged "to exercise their full rights and responsibilities of citizenship." International interests are recognized in the constitution's com-

mitment to promote "the cause of peace and freedom" and
"to aid, assist, and cooperate with free and democratic labor
movements throughout the world." Finally, the constitution
declared the Federation's intent to seek the fulfillment of the
hopes and aspirations of workers "through democratic processes within the framework of our constitutional government
and consistent with our institutions and traditions."

Unions have won acceptance, both nationally and in most
local communities. This recognition is evident in the day-to-
day relationships between workers, their local union officials,
and employers. It is at this basic level of job relations that
the democratic processes of collective bargaining and union-
management joint action to settle disputes and work together
are best demonstrated. At the local and community level,
many unions have formed special committees or groups to

*Technological developments, sometimes called automation,
have replaced old methods of manufacture.*

participate in community activities. Increasing numbers of union members are elected or appointed to local government organizations, such as school boards, city councils, and libraries, and many other civic enterprises.

Unions have always encouraged labor's participation in national affairs and have sought to strengthen labor's influence on national policy. They took an active part in bringing about the establishment of the Department of Labor in 1913. They have strongly supported changes in public policy for dealing with economic crises and modern industrial and social needs, although their interest in such changes has increased in recent years compared with their more limited concern with such problems during the early years of the AFL. During World War I, World War II, and the Korean war, many union officials served on public agencies. More recently, unions and their leaders have participated on various government boards or commissions. Trade union representatives serve on advisory committees to various agencies of Federal and State governments, are elected to public office, and appointed to posts of responsibility.

Collateral Union Activities

Organizing unorganized workers within their jurisdiction continues to be a basic aim of American unions. Historically, of course, this was the principal and most challenging union objective. In this area, many hard-fought struggles occurred. Decades ago, unions and employers had bitter and occasionally bloody disputes, for example, the railroad uprisings of 1877; the Homestead steel strike of 1892; and the conflicts in the anthracite and bituminous coal fields in the early 1900's. In later years, widespread conflicts were avoided, the most serious occurred during the organizing campaigns of the Steel Workers Organizing Committee in 1937 when a number of workers lost their lives and many others were injured.

Today, violent clashes of union organizers or strikers and company guards or strikebreakers are rare, although occasionally a tense struggle is precipitated by an obdurate employer or overly militant or undisciplined union. Organizing activity, however, is still vital to union health and growth, especially in an expanding or a rapidly changing economy. Unions have found special need for organizing activities when employers or industries shift to new localities where unorganized workers in establishments are competing with unionized plants which have higher wages and labor standards. Moreover, the special needs of white-collar people have prompted the labor movement to rethink some of its organizing techniques. Recent movements toward unionization among public employees have resulted in organized labor's involvement. The drive for unionization among farm workers has received the support of unions as well as segments of the public. But, as discussed earlier, the overall result of this union activity has not been particularly successful because union membership, as a percentage of nonagricultural employment, has not grown.

Among the traditional functions of unions was the maintenance of mutual benefit funds. Public social security programs and the supplemental or fringe benefit clauses of collective agreements have reduced the earlier importance of the fraternal benefit functions based on member contributions. A few unions, however, especially among the older crafts, continue to provide sickness, death, old-age, disability, and other benefits. Recently, more and more unions have developed programs to enrich the lives of their older, retired members. In some instances, these programs have included recreational and cultural facilities and the construction of homes or even planned communities.

The AFL–CIO, in addition, is developing programs to encourage union members to appreciate and enjoy the arts through organizing demonstration arts projects in a number of cities.

Educational facilities for their members are provided by many national unions. Certain craft unions support trade schools to help members develop or improve their skills. Educational programs conducted as part of regular union meetings or in special classes or "institutes" have a more general purpose. Some educational work is aimed at training officials in handling union work; accounting methods, for example, for treasurers; or techniques of handling shop grievances for shop stewards who represent the workers in a particular factory or establishment. Classes are provided also to study parliamentary law, public speaking, and American Government and democracy. When, for example, unionization began to expand in the public sector, labor educators had to provide training for the new unionists in this field about the nature and functions of public unions. In addition, unions are directing some of their educational programs toward the young worker. Some of the larger unions maintain extensive training schools that provide formal teaching and field work for candidates for official union positions.

Many universities and colleges now provide special facilities and scholarships for union workers, often in cooperation with unions. The number of such programs has increased greatly in recent years, thus attesting to the importance the union movement attaches to educational activities. In fact, the universities have developed long-term nonresident programs to which unions send members to study an integrated series of subjects. A growing concern has developed for educating top officials and staff of unions. The Brookings Institution in 1963 started a series of "Public Issue Conferences for Selected Union Officials" at which top academic and government officials discussed these issues with top union officials. Moreover, in September 1969, the AFL–CIO inaugurated a National Labor Studies Center in Washington, D.C., which will develop trade union leadership, and carry labor's philosophy to the community through educational programs.

Most unions publish newspapers or journals. These range

in size from leaflets to full-size magazines containing, in addition to union news, special departments and articles on national and international issues. Unions also publish a wide variety of pamphlets and special reports. These, and their radio and television programs, are designed to inform the public, as well as members, of union activities and objectives.

Closely associated with union educational and publications programs are the research activities, which have also expanded greatly in the last three decades. Most of the larger unions now have research departments, although some engage independent specialists to prepare economic briefs and other needed data. The AFL–CIO also maintains a research organization as do some of its departments. The status of research and educational work in the national and international unions and the State Federations was indicated broadly by a study made in 1968. Among the 189 unions reporting to the Bureau of Labor Statistics, 119 unions had research directors and 113 had education directors.

The growth of research and educational facilities reflects the increasing use of factual data on wages, employment, prices, and profits in collective bargaining and in public relations. The increased union testimony and appearances before public agencies and the widespread use of arbitration emphasized the need for accurate data and for clear analysis to meet both management scrutiny and public evaluation of economic issues of interest to unions.

Other types of professional employees frequently found on the staffs of national unions include lawyers, accountants, editors, and others. Occasionally, specialists in such fields as public relations, insurance or health programs, and political action are employed.

Foreign Affairs

The long-standing union interest in world affairs was intensified by World War II and postwar problems. Unions were particularly active in programs for rehabilitating war-torn countries and for reinforcing resistance, especially among workers, to the inroads of communism.

The CIO, late in 1945, joined with labor organizations of 54 countries, including the Soviet Union, to form the World Federation of Trade Unions (WFTU). The AFL refused to join because the Soviet unions were state-dominated, not free unions. It soon became apparent that the Communist unions were determined to make use of the WFTU as a tool of the Communist governments. In 1949, therefore, the CIO and other non-Communist unions withdrew from the WFTU.

Shortly thereafter, the AFL and the CIO agreed to joint participation in a new organization, and on December 7, 1949, the International Confederation of Free Trade Unions

U.S. Secretary of Labor, George P. Shultz, addresses the 53d annual session of the International Labour Organization at Geneva, held in June 1969.

(ICFTU) was formed by delegates from 51 countries representing unions with nearly 50 million members. By the time of the AFL–CIO merger, unions of 76 countries with about 54,500,000 members, were represented in the ICFTU. In 1969, however, the AFL–CIO left the ICFTU because the ICFTU was considering for membership the application of the UAW (which had left the AFL–CIO) and because of AFL–CIO criticism of ICFTU leadership. American unions also joined with the labor movement in Latin American countries in the Inter-American Regional Organization of Workers (ORIT) as part of the ICFTU. Steps were taken to support democratic union movements in critical areas such as Southeast Asia and Africa. Union opposition to communism continued unabated.

The American labor movement has taken an active part in the International Labor Organization (ILO) since 1934, when the United States became a member. Since the merger, the AFL–CIO has continued this activity. The ILO is a world-wide organization—now affiliated with the United Nations—and has 117 member states. Each country has tripartite representation in the ILO and sends delegates from government and national organizations of workers and employers to its annual meetings. The ILO seeks to raise labor standards and improve working conditions by recommendations and conventions subject to ratification by each country; by technical guidance and assistance for increasing productivity, especially in underdeveloped countries; and by the spread of information and mutual understanding on labor-management problems. The Versailles Treaty established the ILO after World War I; Samuel Gompers, then president of the AFL, was one of its founders. It celebrated its fiftieth anniversary in 1969.

Representatives of the labor movement in the United States also have participated in the conduct of labor affairs in the United States Government's Agency for International Development and its predecessor agencies. This agency provides funds and technical assistance to countries throughout the world that want to strengthen their economy. Individuals from union ranks also serve as labor advisers or attaches to American embassies in a number of countries. In this role, they interpret the labor movement in this country to Government officials and workers abroad as well as acquaint United States officials with significant developments in the country in which they are stationed.

But there has been criticism of the AFL–CIO's role in foreign policy from both inside and outside organized labor. Differences over labor's position on foreign policy was one of the reasons that Reuther and the UAW left the AFL–CIO. For example, in 1 year, 1966, Reuther and Meany differed concerning a number of issues: Over the walk-out of the AFL–CIO's delegation at the annual Conference of the ILO when a Communist was elected as presiding officer; over the role of the AFL–CIO in Latin America; over the attitude of organized labor toward the war in Vietnam. Although both Meany, speaking for the majority of the AFL–CIO and Reuther, for the UAW, are firmly opposed to communism, they differed about the degree to which it represents a monolithic, unchanging, unchangeable, universally evil force.

In Perspective: Changes of 85 Years

In 1885, 70 years before the merging of the AFL and the CIO, the labor movement, though small and torn by dissension, was on the eve of formal organization of the AFL. The status of unions and the conditions of workers have improved significantly since then.

As a rule, workers in 1885 worked 10 hours a day. The 6-day week was prevalent except for workers in employment requiring continuous operation. Many workers in these industries had a 7-day schedule. In 1885, premium pay for overtime, paid vacations and holidays, and income upon retirement were almost unknown. By 1970, supplementary benefits were customary, and departures from the prevailing 40-hour, 5-day weekly work schedules found in manufacturing and most nonmanufacturing industries were generally in the direction of shorter working time. Even in trade and service industries, where long hours had tended to persist, substantial progress had been made toward the 40-hour week.

Valid comparisons of wages require consideration of price changes over the years. Although prices have risen substantially, real wages or the purchasing power of the worker's income have increased even more since the mid-1880's. The buying power of wages in 1969 was over 3 times as great as in 1885. In addition, fringe benefits which today are common were virtually nonexistent when Samuel Gompers first embarked on his efforts to build an enduring labor movement in the United States.

Throughout the 70-year period, union members shared the generally prevalent American preference for self-help—individually and by association with their fellow workers. Nevertheless, as bearers of the brunt of competitive wage cutting, sweatshop conditions, depression and unemployment, with other workers, they led the way in support of corrective measures which needed the helping hand of government. Limitations on child labor, protection of women and children as workers, the public regulation of workplaces for maintenance of safety and sanitation, tax reforms, and enforcement of employers' liability for accidents and industrial diseases, gradually were adopted by the States or by the Federal Government. In those early measures, as in the more recent adoption of social security, legal minimum wages, and laws safeguarding basic rights and collective bargaining privileges, labor's influence and labor's gains have been conspicuous.

For the most part, however, the Government's role in times of peace normally remains supplementary to private action—to establish the basic rules and to set minimum standards for wages and labor-management relations. To resolve their problems, workers continue to rely upon their initiative and skills as individuals and upon their group activities and collective strength. Through such efforts unions have grown and gained acceptance by employers and the public as an integral and important part of the country's economic and social structure.

Labor's philosophy has broadened. Adolph Strasser, a union leader in the 1880's, accurately described organized labor's goals then when he declared, "We have no ultimate ends. We are going on from day to day. We are fighting on for immediate objects . . . We are all practical men." This approach still continues but added is the view of a more recent spokesman, Walter Reuther, who argued that "The kind of labor movement we want is not committed to nickel-in-the-pay envelope philosophy. We are building a labor movement, not to patch up the old world so men can starve less often and less frequently, but a labor movement that will remake the world so that the working people will get the benefit of their labor." Both themes, business unionism and social unionism, vie for support within the American labor movement. The differences between them, however, are only a matter of degree, not of kind. Most present-day unions seek to better the conditions of workers through collective bargaining, political action, and social reform—all within the framework of the American democratic society.

Fundamentally, the American labor movement has been pragmatic rather than ideological and as Philip Taft in his "Theories of the Labor Movement" has concluded: "Such a philosophy is not as ostentatious and lacks the architectonic grandeur of philosophical systems such as Marxism. . . . However, the absence of these qualities helps to make the American movement more democratic, tolerant, and flexible. Trade unionism in the United States is a means of protecting the individual against arbitrary rule and raising his standard

Structure of the AFL-CIO

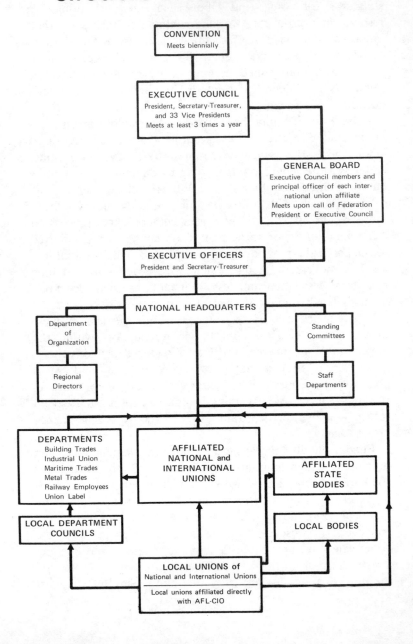

of living. While it may not rank high for philosophy, it deserves high score on the latter count."

APPENDIX

IMPORTANT EVENTS IN AMERICAN LABOR HISTORY

1778   Journeymen printers of New York City combined to demand an increase in wages. After the increase was granted, the organization was abandoned.

1786   The earliest authenticated strike of workers in the United States in a single trade occurred when Philadelphia printers gained a minimum wage of $6 a week.

1791   Philadelphia carpenters struck unsuccessfully in May for a 10-hour day and additional pay for overtime. This was the first recorded strike of workers in the building trades.

1792   The first local craft union formed for collective bargaining was organized by Philadelphia shoemakers. It disbanded in less than a year.

1794   The Federal Society of Journeymen Cordwainers was formed in Philadelphia by the shoeworkers. It lasted until 1806, when it was tried and fined for conspiracy. (See below.)

            The Typographical Society was organized in New York City by the printers. It remained in existence for 10½ years.

1805   A Journeymen Cordwainers' union in New York City included a closed-shop clause in its constitution.

1806   Members of the Philadelphia Journeymen Cordwainers were tried for criminal conspiracy after a strike for higher wages. The charges were (1) combination to raise wages and (2) combination to injure others. The union was found guilty and fined. Bankrupt as a result, the union disbanded. This was the first of several unions to be tried for conspiracy.

1825   The United Tailoresses of New York, a trade

union organization for women only, was formed in New York City.

1827 The Mechanics' Union of Trade Associations, made up of unions of skilled craftsmen in different trades, was formed in Philadelphia. This was the first city central type of organization on record.

1828 The Workingmen's Party, including wage earners, craftsmen, and farmers, was organized in Philadelphia in July. It went out of existence in 1832.

1834 The National Trades' Union was formed in New York City. This was the first attempt toward a national labor federation in the United States. It failed to survive the financial panic of 1837.

1836 The National Cooperative Association of Cordwainers, the first national labor union of a specific craft, was formed in New York City. There is no further record of this organization after 1837. Other trades which formed national organizations within the next few years were the printers, comb makers, carpenters, and hand-loom weavers.

1840 An Executive order issued on March 31 by President Van Buren established a 10-hour day for Federal employees on public works without reduction in pay.

1842 In the case of *Commonwealth* v. *Hunt,* the Massachusetts Court held that labor unions, as such, were legal organizations, and that "a conspiracy must be a combination of two or more persons, by some concerted action, to accomplish some criminal or unlawful purpose, or to accomplish some purpose not in itself criminal or unlawful by criminal or unlawful means." The decision also denied that an attempt to establish a closed shop was unlawful or proof of an unlawful aim.

Massachusetts and Connecticut passed laws prohibiting children from working more than 10 hours a day.

1847   The first State law fixing 10 hours as a legal work-
        day was passed in New Hampshire.

1848   Pennsylvania passed a State child labor law setting
        the minimum age for workers in commercial occupa-
        tions at 12 years. In 1849, the minimum was raised
        to 13 years.

1852   The Typographical Union, the first national orga-
        nization of workers to endure to the present day, was
        formed.

        The first law limiting working hours of women to
        10 hours a day was passed in Ohio.

1859   The Iron Molders' Union, the forerunner of the
        present Molders' and Allied Workers' Union, was
        organized in Philadelphia.

1862   The "Molly Maguires," a secret society of Irish
        miners in the anthracite fields, first came to public
        attention. The "Mollies" were charged with acts of
        terrorism against mine bosses. They went out of
        existence in 1876, when 14 of their leaders were
        imprisoned and 10 were executed.

1863   The present-day Brotherhood of Locomotive Engi-
        neers was founded.

        Laws providing fines and imprisonment for strikers
        preventing other persons from working were passed
        in Illinois and Minnesota.

1866   The National Labor Union, a national association
        of unions, was organized. A federation of trades'
        assemblies rather than of national craft organizations,
        it included radical and reform groups. Drifting into
        social rather than trade union endeavors, it lost
        craftsmen's support and went out of existence in
        1872.

1867   The Knights of St. Crispin was organized on
        March 7 to protect journeymen shoemakers against
        the competition of "green hands" and apprentices in
        the operation of newly introduced machinery in the
        shoe industry. The last vestige of the order disap-

peared in 1878.

1868   The first Federal 8-hour-day law was passed by Congress. It applied only to laborers, workmen, and mechanics employed by or on behalf of the United States Government.

The first State labor bureau was established in Massachusetts.

1869   The Noble Order of the Knights of Labor was organized in Philadelphia. It maintained extreme secrecy until 1878, then began organizing skilled and unskilled workers openly. By winning railroad strikes against the Gould lines, and advancing the program for the 8-hour day, the Knights of Labor gained many followers, claiming over 700,000 members in 1886. It declined rapidly thereafter with the emergence of the AFL.

1870   The first written contract between coal miners and operators was signed on July 29. It provided for a sliding scale of pay, based on the price of coal.

1873   The Brotherhood of Locomotive Firemen and Enginemen was organized.

1874   The Cigar Makers' International Union made first use of the union label.

1878   The Greenback-Labor Party was organized by a fusion of the Greenback Party and Workingmen's Party.

1881   The Federation of Organized Trades and Labor Unions (FOTLU), which later became the American Federation of Labor, was organized in Pittsburgh in November with 107 delegates present. Leaders of 8 national unions attended, including Samuel Gompers, then president of the Cigar Makers' International Union.

The United Brotherhood of Carpenters and Joiners, later to become one of the largest AFL unions, was organized.

1882   The first Labor Day celebration was held in New

York City in September.

1883   The Brotherhood of Railroad Trainmen was orga-
         nized.

1884   A Bureau of Labor was established in the Depart-
         ment of Interior. It later became independent as a
         Department of Labor without Cabinet rank. It then
         was absorbed into a new Department of Commerce
         and Labor, which was created in 1903, where it
         remained until the present Department of Labor was
         established in 1913.

1886   Under the initiative of the Federation of Orga-
         nized Trades and Labor Unions, some 340,000
         workers participated in a movement for an 8-hour
         day.

         The Chicago Haymarket riot, in which one police-
         man was killed and several others wounded, aroused
         public opinion against unionism and radicalism and
         for several years stopped the movement for the 8-
         hour day. The meeting in Haymarket Square had
         been called as a peaceful protest against the killing
         of four strikers and wounding of others during a
         strike for the 8-hour day.

         The American Federation of Labor was organized
         at a convention in Columbus, Ohio, in December as
         successor to the Federation of Organized Trades and
         Labor Unions. Other trade unions and city councils
         which had failed to gain autonomy within the ranks
         of the Knights of Labor also joined the AFL.

1887   The Brotherhood of Maintenance of Way
         Employes was organized.

1888   The first Federal labor relations law was enacted.
         It applied to railroads and provided for arbitration
         and Presidential boards of investigation.

         The International Association of Machinists was
         organized in Atlanta, Ga.

1890   The United Mine Workers was organized in
         Columbus, Ohio.

1892   The Homestead strike by the Amalgamated Association of Iron, Steel & Tin Workers at the Carnegie steel mills in Homestead, Pa., resulted in the death of several strikers and Pinkerton guards. The strike failed and the union was ousted from most mills in the Pittsburgh area.

1894   A strike of the American Railway Union led by Eugene V. Debs against the Pullman Co. was defeated by the use of injunctions and by Federal troops sent into the Chicago area. Debs and several other leaders were imprisoned for violating the injunctions, and the union's effectiveness was destroyed.

1898   Congress passed the Erdman Act, providing for mediation and voluntary arbitration on the railroads, and superseding the law of 1888. The act also made it a criminal offense for railroads to dismiss employees or to discriminate against prospective employees because of their union membership or activity. This portion of the act was subsequently declared invalid by the United States Supreme Court.

1900   The International Ladies' Garment Workers' Union (AFL) was formed.

1901   The International Federation of Trade Unions (then International Secretariat of National Trade Union Centers) was formed on August 21. The AFL affiliated in 1910, disaffiliated in 1921, and reaffiliated in 1937. It remained a member until IFTU was dissolved in 1945.

The Amalgamated Association of Iron, Steel & Tin Workers (AFL) lost 14 union contracts after a 3-month strike against the United States Steel Corp.

The United Textile Workers of America (AFL) was organized.

1902   The United Mine Workers of America ended a 5-month strike on October 21 against anthracite operators, agreeing to arbitration by a Presidential commission. The Anthracite Coal Strike Commission, appointed on October 16, recommended on March 18, 1903, a 10-percent wage increase and conciliation machinery, but denied union recognition.

1903   The Department of Commerce and Labor was created by an act of Congress (act of Feb. 14, 1903, 32 Stat. 825), and its Secretary was made a member of the Cabinet.

1905   The Industrial Workers of the World was organized in Chicago.

The Supreme Court held that a maximum hour law for bakery workers was unconstitutional under the due process clause of the 14th amendment. (*Lochner v. New York.*)

1906   The International Typographical Union (AFL) struck successfully in book and job printing establishments for the 8-hour day, paving the way for extension of shorter hours in the printing trades.

1908   Section 10 of the Erdman Act applying to railroad employees, whereby the "yellow-dog" contract was outlawed and an employer was forbidden to discharge a worker for union membership, was declared unconstitutional. (*U. S. v. Adair.*)

The boycott by the United Hatters of Danbury, Conn., against D. E. Loewe and Co. was held to be in restraint of trade under the Sherman Anti-Trust Act. In January 1915, the individual union members were held responsible for the union's acts and were assessed damages and costs totaling $252,000. This was the first application of the treble damage provision of the act to the labor union.

1909   The 2-month strike of the International Ladies' Garment Workers' Union (AFL) was settled by providing preferential union hiring, a board of grievances, and a board of arbitration. This laid the foundation for the impartial chairman method of settling labor disputes.

1911   The Supreme Court upheld an injunction ordering
            the AFL to eliminate the Bucks Stove and Range
            Co. from its unfair list and to cease to promote an
            unlawful boycott. A contempt charge against union
            leaders, including AFL President Samuel Gompers,
            was dismissed on technical grounds. (*Gompers v.
            Bucks Stove and Range Co.*)

            The Triangle Waist Co. fire in New York on
            March 25, which caused the death of 146 workers,
            led to establishment of the New York Factory Inves-
            tigating Commission on June 30, and eventual
            improvement in factory conditions.

1912   Massachusetts adopted the first minimum wage act
            for women and minors.

            The (Walsh) Commission on Industrial Relations
            was created to investigate industrial unrest. In 1916,
            it rendered a comprehensive series of reports on the
            status of labor-management relations.

1913   The United States Department of Labor was
            established by law. It included the Bureau of Labor
            Statistics (created in 1884 as the Bureau of Labor,
            see above), the Bureau of Immigration and Naturali-
            zation (created in 1891), and the Children's Bureau
            (created in 1912). Power was given the Secretary of
            Labor to "act as mediator and to appoint commis-
            sioners of conciliation in labor disputes," and in
            1918, the Conciliation Service was established as a
            separate division of the Department. William B.
            Wilson, a trade unionist and Member of Congress,
            became the first Secretary of Labor.

            The Newlands Act set up a Board of Mediation
            and Conciliation to handle railroad disputes.

1914   The Clayton Act was approved, limiting the use of
            injunctions in labor disputes and providing that pick-
            eting and other union activities shall not be consid-
            ered unlawful.

            On December 1, the President appointed the Colorado Coal Commission which investigated the Ludlow Massacre and labor conditions in Colorado coal mines following an unsuccessful strike by the United Mine Workers.

The Amalgamated Clothing Workers was formed by a seceding group of the United Garment Workers (AFL).

1915   The LaFollette Seamen's Act was approved on March 4, regulating conditions of employment for maritime workers.

1916   A Federal child labor law was enacted (declared unconstitutional on June 3, 1918); followed by act of February 24, 1919 (declared unconstitutional on May 15, 1922); followed by a child labor amendment to the Constitution on June 2, 1924. Only 28 of the necessary 36 States ratified the amendment.

The Adamson Act, providing a basic 8-hour day on railroads, was enacted to eliminate a threatened nationwide railroad strike.

1917   A strike led by the Industrial Workers of the World (IWW) in the copper mines of Bisbee, Ariz., was ended when the sheriff deported 1,200 strikers.

The President appointed a mediation commission, headed by the Secretary of Labor, to adjust wartime labor difficulties.

The "yellow-dog" contract was upheld and union efforts to organize workers party to such contract were held to be unlawful. (*Hitchman Coal & Coke Co. v. Mitchell.*)

1918   The Federal Government took control of the railroads from December 1917 until March 1, 1920, under existing Federal legislation which provided for Government railroad operation in wartime.

The President named the Secretary of Labor as War Labor Administrator on January 4.

The President created the National War Labor Board on April 8 "to settle by mediation and conciliation controversies * * * in fields of production necessary for the effective conduct of the war." It went out of existence in May 1919.

The minimum wage law of the District of Columbia was approved September 19. (Declared unconstitutional on April 9, 1923.)

1919   Led by President Gompers of the AFL, a commission created by the Peace Conference at its second plenary session in January recommended the inclusion in the Peace Treaty of labor clauses creating an International Labor Organization.

The United Mine Workers of America struck against bituminous-coal operators on November 1. In December, the union agreed to arbitration by a Presidential commission. The Bituminous Coal Commission appointed by the President on December 19 awarded a 27-percent wage increase, but denied the 6-hour day and 5-day week.

1920   The AFL Iron and Steel Organizing Committee ended an unsuccessful 3½-month strike in the steel industry on January 8 after most of the strikers had drifted back to work.

The Women's Bureau was established in the Department of Labor by act of Congress.

The Kansas Court of Industrial Relations provided the first experiment in compulsory arbitration in the United States. (Held unconstitutional in part in 1923.)

The Transportation Act provided for a tripartite Railroad Labor Board and terminated Federal control of railroads on March 1.

1921   The Supreme Court held that nothing in the Clayton Act legalized secondary boycotts or protected unions against injunctions brought against them for conspiracy in restraint of trade. (*Duplex Printing Press v. Deering.*)

An act restricting the immigration of aliens into

the United States and establishing the national origin quota system was approved.

The International Seamen's Union (AFL) and Marine Engineers Beneficial Association (AFL) lost a 52-day strike against wage reductions.

The President's Conference on Unemployment placed the main responsibility for unemployment relief upon local communities.

The Arizona law forbidding injunctions in labor disputes and permitting picketing was held unconstitutional under the 14th amendment. (*Truax v. Corrigan.*)

1922   The United Mine Workers was held not responsible for local strike action, and strike action was held not a conspiracy to restrain commerce within the Sherman Anti-Trust Act. Labor unions, however, were held suable for their acts. (*Coronado Coal Co. v. UMWA.*)

A 2½-month unsuccessful nationwide strike of railway shopmen against wage reductions began July 1.

1924   Samuel Gompers, president of the AFL, died on December 13.

1926   The Railway Labor Act, passed on May 20, required employers to bargain collectively and not discriminate against their employees for joining a union. The act also provided for the settlement of railway labor disputes through mediation, voluntary arbitration, and factfinding boards.

1927   The Longshoremen's and Harbor Workers' Compensation Act was enacted.

The Journeymen Stone Cutters' action in trying to prevent purchase of nonunion cut stone was held to be an illegal restraint of interstate commerce. (*Bedford Cut Stone Co. v. Journeymen Stone Cutters' Association, et al.*)

1929   The Hawes-Cooper Act governing the shipment of

convict-made goods in interstate commerce was approved.

The Communist-inspired Trade Union Unity League was formed in September. It was dissolved in 1935.

1930   The Railway Labor Act's prohibition of employer interference or coercion in the choice of bargaining representatives was upheld by the Supreme Court. (*Texas & N. O. R. Co. v. Brotherhood of Railway Clerks.*)

1931   The Davis-Bacon Act provided for the payment of prevailing wage rates to laborers and mechanics employed by contractors and subcontractors on public construction.

1932   The Anti-Injunction (Norris-La Guardia) Act prohibited Federal injunctions in labor disputes, except as specified, and outlawed "yellow-dog" contracts.

Wisconsin adopted the first unemployment insurance act in the United States.

1933   Section 7(a) of the National Industrial Recovery Act provided that every NRA code and agreement should guarantee the right of employees to organize and bargain collectively through their representatives without interference, restraint, or coercion by employers. (Title I of act declared unconstitutional in *Schecter v. U.S.* on May 27, 1935.)

The Wagner-Peyser Act created the United States Employment Service in the Department of Labor.

1934   The first National Labor Legislation Conference was called by Secretary of Labor Frances Perkins to obtain closer Federal-State cooperation in working out a sound national labor legislation program. Annual conferences were held until 1955.

The United States joined the International Labor Organization.

1935   The National Labor Relations (Wagner) Act

established the first national labor policy of protecting the right of workers to organize and to elect their representatives for collective bargaining.

The Bituminous Coal Conservation (Guffey) Act was passed to stabilize the industry and to improve labor conditions. (Labor relations provisions declared unconstitutional on May 18, 1936.)

The Federal Social Security Act was approved August 14.

The Committee for Industrial Organization (later the Congress of Industrial Organizations) was formed on November 9 by several AFL international unions and officials to foster industrial unionism.

1936   In the first large "sitdown" strike, the United Rubber Workers (CIO) won recognition at Goodyear Tire & Rubber Co.

The Anti-Strikebreaker (Byrnes) Act declared it unlawful "to transport or aid in transporting strikebreakers in interstate or foreign commerce."

The Public Contracts (Walsh-Healey) Act established labor standards on Government contracts, including minimum wages, overtime compensation for hours in excess of 8 a day or 40 a week, child and convict labor provisions, and health and safety requirements.

1937   General Motors Corp. agreed to recognize the United Automobile Workers (CIO) as the bargaining agent for its members, to drop injunction proceedings against strikers, not to discriminate against union members, and to establish grievance procedures.

United States Steel Corp. recognized the Steel Workers Organizing Committee as the bargaining agent for its members. A 10-percent wage increase and an 8-hour day and 40-hour week were negotiated.

The National Labor Relations Act was held constitutional. (*NLRB v. Jones & Laughlin Steel Corp.*)

Ten people were killed and 80 were wounded in a Memorial Day clash between police and the members of the Steel Workers Organizing Committee at the plant of the Republic Steel Co. in South Chicago.

The Railroad Retirement Act of 1937 was approved, followed by the Carriers Taxing Act of 1937. (Similar laws of June 27, 1934, and August 29, 1935, had been declared unconstitutional.)

The 5-week "Little Steel' strike was broken on July 1 when Inland Steel employees returned to work without union recognition or other gains.

The National Apprenticeship Act was passed, establishing the Bureau of Apprenticeship in the U.S. Department of Labor.

1938   The Merchant Marine Act of 1936 was amended to provide a Federal Maritime Labor Board.

The Fair Labor Standards Act provided a 25-cent minimum wage and time and a half for hours over 40 a week. (Amended 1949, 1955, 1961, 1963, and 1966.)

The Railroad Unemployment Insurance (Crosser-Wheeler) Act was passed.

1940   A sitdown strike was held not to be an illegal restraint of commerce under the Sherman Anti-Trust Act in the absence of intent to impose market controls. (*Apex Hosiery Co. v. Leader.*)

1941   Actions by the Carpenters' union in jurisdictional disputes were held to be protected by the Clayton Act from prosecution under the Sherman Anti-Trust Act. These actions were construed in light of Congress' definition of "labor dispute" in the Norris-La Guardia Act. (*U.S. v. Hutcheson.*)

The UAW (CIO) won recognition at Ford Motor Co. after a 10-day strike. The union and the company signed a union-shop agreement—the first with a major automobile manufacturer.

The President on December 24 announced a no-strike pledge by the AFL and CIO for the duration of the war.

1942   The United Steelworkers of America was organized. It replaced the Steel Workers Organizing Committee, which was first established by the CIO in 1936.

The President established the National War Labor Board to determine procedures for settling disputes.

The NWLB laid down the "Little Steel" formula for wartime wage adjustments (i.e., based on a 15-percent rise in living costs from January 1, 1941, to May 1, 1942).

The Stabilization Act authorized the President to stabilize wages and salaries, as far as practicable, based on September 15, 1942, levels.

1943   The President by an Executive order created a Committee on Fair Employment Practices, empowering it to "conduct hearings, make findings of fact, and take appropriate steps to obtain elimination" of "discrimination in the employment of any person in war industries or in Government by reason of race, creed, color, or national origin."

The War Labor Disputes (Smith-Connally) Act, passed over the President's veto, authorized plant seizure if needed to avoid interference with the war effort.

1944   The Railway Labor Act, authorizing a labor union chosen by a majority to represent a craft, was held to require union protection of the minority in that class. Discrimination against certain members on ground of race was held enjoinable. (*Steele v. Louisville & Nashville Railroad.*)

1945   The CIO affiliated with the newly formed World Federation of Trade Unions. (It withdrew in 1949.) The AFL, which held that the labor organizations of Soviet Russia were not "free or democratic," did not affiliate with the WFTU.

The President's National Labor-Management Conference convened in Washington, D. C., but produced few tangible results.

1946   The United Steelworkers (CIO) ended a 1-month strike and established a "first round" wage pattern increase of 18½ cents an hour.

The Employment Act of 1946 committed the Government to take all practicable measures to promote maximum employment, production, and purchasing power.

The United Automobile Workers (CIO) ended a 3½-month strike against General Motors Corp. by negotiating an hourly wage increase of 18½ cents, after a Presidential factfinding board had recommended 19½ cents.

Locomotive Engineers (Ind.) and Railroad Trainmen (Ind.) ended a national 2-day strike following an injunction and under threat of legislation to draft the workers. They accepted the 18½-cent-an-hour increase recommended by the President.

The UMWA bituminous-coal miners won a health and welfare fund from the Federal Government, which had seized the mines. The fund was to be financed from payments by operators of 5 cents a ton of coal produced.

The President provided for the termination of all wartime wage and salary controls.

1947   The Norris-La Guardia Act prohibition against issuance of injunctions in labor disputes was held inapplicable to the Government as an employer. (*U. S. v. John L. Lewis.*)

The Portal-to-Portal Act was approved, "to relieve employers and the Government from potential liability * * * in 'portal-to-portal' claims."

The Labor Management Relations (Taft-Hartley) Act was passed (June 23) over the President's veto.

1948   Mississippi became the 48th State to enact workmen's compensation legislation.

The President appointed the Commission on Labor Relations in the Atomic Energy Installations, which, on April 18, 1949, recommended establishment of a panel to protect free collective bargaining in atomic plants.

The Federal Government's first national conference on industrial safety met in Washington, D. C.

1949   The Fair Labor Standards Act (1938) was amended to raise the minimum wage of workers covered by the act to 75 cents an hour. Child labor was directly prohibited for the first time.

The United States Supreme Court, by denying review of a lower court's action, upheld a decision that the Labor Management Relations Act requires employers to bargain with unions on retirement plans. (*Inland Steel Co. v. United Steelworkers of America.*)

Settlement of a steel industry-United Steelworkers (CIO) strike on the basis of noncontributory $100 monthly pensions at age 65, plus death, sickness, and accident benefits, followed a recommendation by a Presidential factfinding board that employers contribute 6 cents an hour toward pensions and 4 cents an hour toward social insurance for each worker.

The CIO anti-Communist drive culminated in expulsion of two unions at its annual convention. Trial and expulsion of nine other unions followed early in 1950.

The International Union of Electrical, Radio and Machine Workers was founded at the CIO convention following the expulsion of the United Electrical, Radio and Machine Workers.

Free, democratic trade unions of various countries, including the CIO in the United States, withdrew early in 1949 from the World Federation of Trade

Unions, which had become Communist dominated.

A new worldwide labor organization—the International Confederation of Free Trade Unions (IFCTU)—with the AFL, CIO, and United Mine Workers participating, was formed at a meeting in December at London, England, of labor representatives from 51 countries.

1950   A 5-year contract with no reopening provisions was negotiated by the United Automobile Workers (CIO) and the General Motors Corp. It provided for pensions, automatic cost-of-living wage adjustments, guaranteed annual increases, and a modified union shop.

The AFL launched a yearlong series of observances commemorating the centennial of Samuel Gompers' birth on January 27, 1850.

A United Labor Policy Committee composed of representatives of the AFL, CIO, and railroad unions was formed in December for the purpose of presenting labor's views to the Government on problems arising from the national emergency. The AFL withdrew from the committee in August 1951, thereby dissolving the group.

The Defense Production Act, authorizing the President to curb inflation and promote defense production, was approved September 8.

1951   The International Association of Machinists reaffiliated with the AFL in January after being independent since 1945 due to jurisdictional disputes. In August, the American Federation of Hosiery Workers, formerly an affiliate of the AFL United Textile Workers, rejoined the AFL as a separate union.

The Inter-American Regional Workers Organization (ORIT) of the International Confederation of Free Trade Unions was established at a meeting in Mexico City in January. It claimed to represent 17 million workers in North, South, and Central America.

Labor representatives withdrew in February from all participation in the Government's mobilization and stabilization program in protest over what they felt was labor's secondary role in its operation. They voted to return in April after being given a stronger voice in policy-making.

The CIO participated with the AFL as part of the United States delegation to the International Labor Conference of the ILO for the first time since 1946.

The first amendment to the Taft-Hartley Act, permitting negotiations of union-shop agreements without previous polls of employees, became law in October. The union shop for workers on the Nation's rail and air lines had previously been approved under the National (Railway) Mediation Act in January.

1952   A Presidential emergency board, in February, recommended agreement on the union shop between the railroads and nonoperating railroad unions representing about 1 million workers.

Three unions of railroad operating employees and the carriers reached an agreement on wage increases and working rules in May. Federal operation of the railroads was brought to an end, after being in effect since August 1950.

A strike of nearly 8 weeks' duration ended in July when the United Steelworkers of America (CIO) signed agreements with basic steel producers employing about 500,000 workers. Following the companies' rejection of Wage Stabilization Board recommendations, the Government seized the steel industry. The strike began after a district court granted an injunction restraining the seizure order, but it was halted at the request of the President pending review of the decision by the United States

Supreme Court. The strike was resumed after the Supreme Court held that the President exceeded his constitutional powers when he ordered the seizure.

Wage and price controls were extended until April 30, 1953, by a revised Defense Production Act. The Act established a new tripartite Wage Stabilization Board without disputes-settlement authority.

Presidents of two principal labor federations, Philip Murray of the CIO and William Green of the AFL, died in November. The AFL Executive Council elevated George Meany, former secretary-treasurer of the Federation, to the presidency. Walter P. Reuther, president of the United Automobile Workers, was named president of the CIO by the CIO convention.

Martin P. Durkin, president of the Plumbers and Pipe Fitters Union, was designated by President-elect Eisenhower to be Secretary of Labor in the new Cabinet. Mr. Durkin was the first active union official and the fourth unionist to be named Secretary of Labor since the establishment of the Department of Labor in 1913.

1953   President Eisenhower on February 6 ordered the end of Government controls on wages and salaries. At the same time, he ordered prices decontrolled on a considerable list of consumer goods. All remaining price controls were terminated on March 17.

The Supreme Court of the United States upheld the right of the International Typographical Union (AFL) to compel a newspaper to pay for the setting of type not used, and of the American Federation of Musicians (AFL) to demand that a local "standby" orchestra be employed when a traveling orchestra was hired for an engagement. The Court said that neither practice violated the "featherbedding" ban in the Labor Management Relations (Taft-Hartley) Act.

Martin P. Durkin resigned as Secretary of Labor on September 10. On October 8, President Eisenhower appointed James P. Mitchell, who had served as Assistant Secretary of the Army for Manpower, to succeed Mr. Durkin.

The American Federation of Labor and the Congress of Industrial Organizations, meeting in their respective conventions, approved a no-raiding pact to extend for 2 years from January 1, 1954. The agreement was binding only upon those member unions accepting it. Both organizations hailed the pact as the first step towards organic unity.

The convention of the American Federation of Labor on September 22 revoked the 60-year-old charter of the International Longshoremen's Association, charging corruption within the union. A new union was immediately chartered by the AFL. A bitter struggle for representation in the east coast longshore industry, between the old ILA and the newly chartered AFL union, took place on the docks, in the courts, and in NLRB hearing rooms during the last 3 months of 1953. (Following a representation election in which the AFL union was defeated, the unaffiliated ILA was certified by the NLRB in August 1954 as collective bargaining agent for the dock workers.)

1954   Organic unity between the AFL and CIO moved swiftly toward accomplishment as a result of action taken during the year. A "no-raiding" agreement was activated in June. After a series of meetings, unity committees of the two federations agreed in October upon merger without resolving in advance the jurisdiction of competing AFL and CIO unions. (Unity committees and the executive boards of the AFL and CIO approved the terms of the merger in February 1955.)

Major railroads and the unions of nonoperating

railroad workers negotiated an agreement to provide comprehensive health and insurance benefits, to be financed by contributions from employers and workers.[1] This action raised the total number of workers than covered by some type of health, welfare, and pension plan under collective bargaining to approximately 12 million.

In his message to Congress on January 11, 1954, President Eisenhower recommended that Congress initiate a thorough study of welfare and pension funds with a view to protecting and conserving these funds. Investigations by State and Federal committees, which uncovered instances of fraud and mismanagement on the part of local union officials in the administration of welfare and pension funds, prompted the AFL and CIO to act to end such abuses and to establish standards for fund management and control.

Unions increased their efforts to end, or prevent the passage of, State "right to work" laws, which ban union membership as a qualification for employment. These laws were in effect in 17 States at the end of 1954.

Proposals for guaranteed annual employment or wage plans were developed by the United Automobile Workers, the Steelworkers, the Electrical Workers, and the Rubber Workers.

The AFL and CIO resumed active participation in the work of the U. S. Foreign Operations Administration in the revitalized Office of Labor Affairs, with labor missions and advisory posts abroad. American unions also continued to participate actively in international labor affairs through their affiliation with the International Confederation of Free Trade Unions (ICFTU).

[1] Employers took over full cost in 1955.

1955 The Fair Labor Standards Act was amended to raise the minimum wage for covered workers from 75 cents to $1 an hour, effective March 1, 1956.

In June, the Ford Motor Co. and the United Auto Workers (CIO) negotiated a new 3-year agreement which established a supplementary unemployment compensation plan financed by company contributions of 5 cents an hour. Payments under the plan to eligible laid-off workers were to start on June 1, 1956. By the end of 1955, similar plans were negotiated for more than a million workers including the remainder of the auto industry.

The founding of the American Federation of Labor and Congress of Industrial Organizations (AFL-CIO) on December 5, 1955, brought into one center unions representing approximately 16 million workers—over 85 percent of the membership claimed by all unions in the United States. The last conventions of the separate organizations, held on December 1 and 2, approved the merger agreement, a new constitution, and an implementation agreement designed to combine the two federations without dissolving either organization. The first convention of the AFL–CIO elected its president (George Meany), secretary-treasurer (William F. Schnitzler), and 27 vice presidents, 17 of whom had been proposed by the AFL and 10 by the CIO. Under the constitution, these 29 officers constitute the Executive Council, the governing body between the biennial conventions.

Mergers among AFL–CIO affiliates, while encouraged, were not to be dictated by the Federation; conflicts among unions competing in the same field were likewise to be adjusted voluntarily. Existing State, territorial, and local bodies previously established by the CIO and the AFL were required to merge within 2 years. The constitution provided for an industrial union department to promote the interests of unions organized on an industrial basis. It was organized during the convention week with 69 affiliated unions, including 38 former AFL unions.

1956   The AFL–CIO and its affiliated unions began what was expected to be a slow adjustment to the needs of a united labor organization. In the first year of unity, former AFL and CIO State labor organizations merged in 19 States. The Brotherhood of Locomotive Firemen and Enginemen—unaffiliated throughout its 83-year history—joined the AFL–CIO in September. Although several international unions proposed and discussed mergers, only a few were actually carried out. On the other hand, a number of unions signed mutual assistance pacts or no-raiding agreements. No large-scale organizing program was attempted. The Federation's Ethical Practices Committee recommended to the Executive Council, after hearings, that three unions (the Allied Industrial Workers, the Laundry Workers, and the Distillery Workers) should show cause why they should not be suspended because of domination by "corrupt" influences in the administration of employee welfare funds.

In collective bargaining, renewed interest in deferred wage increases and in plans permitting wages to be adjusted to changes in living costs was evident. A trend to long-term agreements, which had been developing in recent years, became more pronounced. Supplementary unemployment benefit plans, introduced in 1955, became more prevalent but were limited to several major industries. Three-year agreements in the steel industry, reached after a 5-week strike in July, provided for an immediate wage increase, annual increases, semiannual wage escalation, the establishment of supplementary unemployment benefit plans, and other benefits.

Amendments to the Federal Social Security Act

provided that disabled industrial workers may qualify for disability benefits at age 50, and women may retire at age 62 with reduced benefits. Railroad Retirement Act benefits were increased by 10 percent. Benefits were increased and the waiting period lowered for disabled workers coming under the Longshoremen's and Harbor Workers' Compensation Act. Benefits for Federal employees under the civil service retirement system were increased. Old-age and survivors' insurance benefits were extended to additional self-employed persons and the uniformed services.

The United Mine Workers of America (Ind.) in June dedicated 10 new hospitals to serve miners, their families, and communities in Virginia, West Virginia, and Kentucky. The cost of the project was financed by the UMWA Retirement and Welfare Fund, to which bituminous-coal operators pay 40 cents for each ton of coal mined under union contract conditions. Five of the hospitals were sold in 1963.

1957 The December 1957 biennial convention of the AFL–CIO expelled the Teamsters, Bakery Workers, and Laundry Workers, with a combined membership of approximately 1.6 million, on charges of domination by corrupt influences. This action followed upon a refusal on the part of the 3 unions to accept the corrective recommendation of the Executive Council. Of the unions for which corrective action was recommended, the Distillery Workers remained on probation and the United Textile Workers was restored to good standing in the Federation. The Allied Industrial Workers had complied with the Executive Council order prior to the convention.

Three formerly independent railroad unions became affiliated with the AFL–CIO during 1957: The Brotherhood of Railroad Trainmen, the American Train Dispatchers Association, and the American Railway Supervisors Association.

1958   Investigation of unions whose officials were suspected of corrupt practices was continued throughout much of the year by the Senate Select Committee on Improper Activities in the Labor or Management Field. The AFL–CIO took disciplinary action against officers of affiliated unions who refused to answer questions for fear of self-incrimination.

Federal legislation passed during 1958 included a Welfare and Pension Plans Disclosure Act, which requires administrators of all health, insurance, pension, and supplementary unemployment compensation plans covering more than 25 workers (amended 1962) to file with the Secretary of Labor descriptions and annual financial reports, to be available for public inspection. Reports must also be made available for plan participants. Other laws included one for optional Federal loans to States for a temporary 50-percent extension of unemployment payments to workers who had exhausted their benefits under Federal and State Programs; and another for the increase of Federal old-age, survivors, and disability benefits by about 7 percent.

1959   The Labor-Management Reporting and Disclosure Act of 1959, designed to eliminate improper activities by labor or management, was passed by the Congress and signed into law by the President on September 14. The act provides certain protection for the rights of labor organization members; provides for the filing of reports describing the organization, financial dealings, and business practices of labor organizations, their officers and employees, certain employers, labor relations consultants, and unions in trusteeship; safeguards union election procedures; sets standards for the handling of union funds; amends the Taft-Hartley law to eliminate the "no-man's land" in NLRB cases; closes previously existing loopholes in the protection against secondary boycotts; and limits organizational and jurisdictional picketing. The statute is administered by the Department of Labor. The National Labor Relations Board administers portions of the statute amending the Taft-Hartley Act.

The longest major strike ever to take place in the steel industry began on July 15. Attempts to resolve the dispute through negotiation continued until October 21, when the national emergency provisions of the Taft-Hartley Act were invoked. After an unsuccessful attempt on the part of a board of inquiry to promote a settlement, a back-to-work injunction was issued. After a court battle over the constitutionality and applicability of the injunction, the Supreme Court upheld the injunction on November 7, the 116th day of the strike. Workers then returned to their jobs for the 80-day "cooling off" period. (Negotiations were successfully completed and new contracts signed early in January 1960.)

The third biennial convention of the AFL-CIO was held in San Francisco in September. Steps were taken for greater internal unity and the settlement of jurisdictional disputes. The convention revealed the Federation on the defensive on legislative, political, and economic fronts.

1960   The Nation's railroads and the five operating brotherhoods agreed to refer their longstanding dispute involving work rules and practices to a tripartite Presidential commission of 15 members for study and recommendations.

An agreement which opened the way to relaxation of restrictive working rules and the increased use of labor-saving equipment on the waterfront was signed by the Pacific Maritime Association and the International Longshoremen's and Warehousemen's Union.

In return for the union's acceptance of the changes, the association agreed to contribute $5 million a year to a fund to provide each of the 15,000 registered longshoremen $7,920 upon retirement at age 65 with 25 years of service, and to guarantee union members certain minimum weekly earnings and no layoffs as a result of decreased work opportunities under the new contract provisions. However, the fund would not protect longshoremen from reduced earnings resulting from a decline in business.

Arthur J. Goldberg, general counsel to the United Steelworkers and special counsel of the AFL–CIO, was appointed by President-elect John F. Kennedy to be Secretary of Labor.

1961   President Kennedy established an Advisory Committee on Labor-Management Policy with 21 members from business, labor, and the public, to make recommendations that might promote industrial peace and sound wage and price policies. Another committee established during the year by Executive order was the 11-man tripartite Missile Sites Labor Commission, organized to resolve labor problems at missile and space installations. A 3-man board composed of representatives of the U.S. Departments of Labor and Commerce and a public arbitrator was set up to consider the foreign flag issue raised by the maritime unions.

Social Security amendments, which became effective August 1, increased the minimum monthly insurance benefits from $33 to $40, extended coverage to additional State and local government employees, permitted men to retire at age 62 on reduced benefits (previously extended only to women), increased aged widows' benefits by 10 percent, and liberalized the insured status and the retirement test. Contributions rates were raised, beginning in 1962, by one-eighth of 1 percent for employers and employees.

Amendments to the Fair Labor Standards Act went into effect September 3, extending coverage to about 3.6 million workers, mostly in retail trade and construction. Minimum wage rates of workers already covered were increased from $1.00 to $1.15 an hour, to be raised to $1.25 September 1963. Newly covered workers began with a $1.00 minimum in September 1961. They reached a $1.15 rate September 1964 and a $1.25 rate September 1965. They were brought gradually under the overtime provisions of the act until they received time and one-half pay for hours after 40 per week by September 1965.

In July, the International Brotherhood of Teamsters, which had been expelled by the AFL–CIO in 1957, held its first convention since the expulsion, following the release of the union from Federal court surveillance and monitor control. Constitutional changes centralized authority in the international officers, increased dues, and expanded the union's jurisdiction.

The Southern Pacific Railroad and the Order of Railroad Telegraphers negotiated an agreement guaranteeing each telegrapher his job or equivalent wages during his lifetime.

The fourth biennial convention of the AFL–CIO, held in December, approved a constitutional amendment setting up a procedure for the peaceful resolution of jurisdictional disputes, a problem that had been disruptive since the 1955 merger. Constructive steps were also taken by the convention in the campaign to eliminate all vestiges of racial discrimination in the ranks of the AFL–CIO. Organization of the unorganized was declared to be the major unfinished business of the American labor movement, and a new committee on organization was provided for, to develop programs and policies for the Federation.

1962   Major changes in work rules for railroad employees were recommended by a Presidential railroad commission. Elimination of firemen on diesel locomotives in freight and yard services, lowering of mandatory retirement age, reformation of the pay structure, and use of binding arbitration to settle disputes over technological changes and over the size of train crews were suggested. No final decision was reached by year's end.

The Manpower Development and Training Act was approved on March 15, 1962. It requires the Federal Government to determine manpower requirements and resources and to "deal with the problems of unemployment resulting from automation and technological changes and other types of persistent unemployment." The act is administered by the Secretary of Labor and the Secretary of Health, Education, and Welfare.

Secretary of Labor Arthur J. Goldberg was nominated to the post of Associate Justice of the United States Supreme Court on August 29. Willard Wirtz, Under Secretary of Labor, was named to succeed him as Secretary.

Federal employees' unions were granted the right to bargain collectively with Government agencies under an Executive order signed January 17. The order guarantees to unions of Federal workers certain rights of organization, consultation, and processing of grievances.

The Welfare and Pension Plans Disclosure Act of 1958 was amended.

1963   An Atlantic and gulf coasts strike by the International Longshoremen's Association ended January 25, after a 34-day strike following the expiration of a Taft-Hartley injunction. The settlement was based upon recommendations of a special Presidential board, and included provision for a study by the Department of Labor "of the problems of manpower utilization, job security, and all other related issues which affect the longshore industry."

Wyoming passed a "right to work" law, becoming the 20th State to have legislation which forbids contracts requiring an employee to become or remain a member of a labor union as a condition of employment. Both the agency shop and union shop are banned.

The 50th anniversary of the U.S. Department of Labor was celebrated on March 4.

Two long newspaper stoppages, 114 days in New York and 126 days in Cleveland, ended March 31 and April 5, respectively.

The Equal Pay Act of 1963 was signed by the President on June 10. This act prohibits wage differentials based on sex after June 10, 1964, for workers covered by the Fair Labor Standards Act.

The struggle to arrive at a satisfactory solution of the longstanding railroad dispute involving operating railroad workers continued throughout the year. Negotiations failed to produce any concrete results. On August 28, Congress passed legislation calling for arbitration of the two principal issues: the use of firemen on diesel locomotives in freight and yard service, and the makeup of train crews. The report of the arbitrators, issued on November 26, provided for the gradual elimination of firemen in 90 percent of freight and yard service. The crew "consist issue" was returned to the unions and carriers for further negotiations, and arbitration, if necessary.

The fifth biennial convention of the AFL–CIO was held in New York City, November 14–20. Domestic and international problems of concern to the labor movement were the primary topics of interest, with civil rights, unemployment, and automation receiving the most attention. Some 250 resolutions were adopted, many of them including lengthy statements of the AFL–CIO reasoning and position on the various issues.

1964   The 4½-year dispute between the railroads and operating brotherhoods over work rules and other collective bargaining issues ended when final agreement was reached on all issues not resolved by the arbitration award of November 1963. The Brotherhood of Locomotive Firemen and Enginemen ratified the agreement on June 25, the last of the five operating unions to do so.

The Civil Rights Act of 1964 was signed by the President on July 2, to become effective a year later. Title VII—Equal Employment Opportunity—bars discrimination on the basis of race, color, religion, sex, or national origin in hiring, apprenticeship, compensation, and terms, conditions, or privileges of employment, and in union membership. An Equal Employment Opportunity Commission was charged with investigating and adjudicating complaints under this title.

The Lithographers (Ind.) and the Photo-Engravers (AFL–CIO) agreed to merge into a single union, effective September 7. New York Local 1 of the Lithographers refused to participate in the merger.

The inability on the part of the International Longshoremen's Association and the New York Shipping Association to agree on the terms of a new contract and the union's rejection of recommendations made by a special Board of Mediation on the basis of a Department of Labor study of manpower utilization and job security led to a strike of all east coast and gulf coast ports on October 1. The strike was immediately halted when the President invoked the 80-day injunction provisions of the Taft-Hartley Act. This was the sixth application of the national emergency provisions of the act to east coast longshoring.

The Economic Opportunity Act of 1964 was signed into law on August 20. The measure provides for work and education programs, loans to low-income farmers and businessmen, and various other national and community antipoverty programs.

Although new master contracts between the United Automobile Workers and the principal automobile manufacturers were signed in September and October, the negotiation of plant supplementary contracts later resulted in widespread strikes. Significantly liberalized early retirement benefits were among changes provided by the new contracts.

1965   The longshore dispute erupted into a strike beginning January 11, after New York longshoremen voted down an agreement reached just before the injunction expired (see entry in 1964). The strike lasted about a month in major ports, but all east and gulf coast ports were not back to work until another month had elapsed.

The Hosiery Workers union was formally dissolved after 50 years of existence, and its members were absorbed by the Textile Workers Union of America (AFL–CIO). Once a union of 50,000 members, the Hosiery Workers union had declined to around 5,000.

Paul Jennings was installed as president of the International Union of Electrical Workers (AFL-CIO) following his defeat of James B. Carey, president of the union since its organization 15 years before.

David J. McDonald, president of the United Steelworkers of America since 1953, was defeated by I. W. Abel in a closely contested election. Only about 10,000 votes separated the contestants, with more than 600,000 votes cast.

Bargaining for new steel contracts, delayed by the Steelworkers election and postponed until September

1 by agreement of the parties, resulted in an agreement emphasizing early retirement and higher pension benefits. The value of the package conformed to the Government's wage-price guideposts, as set forth in the President's annual Economic Report since 1962.

Repeal of Section 14(b) of the Taft-Hartley Act failed passage during the 1st session of the 89th Congress when a vote on H.R. 77 for repeal was blocked by a Senate filibuster. This section of the Act permits States to pass so-called "right to work" laws, which prohibit the requirement of membership in a labor organization as a condition of employment. Its repeal has long been a prime goal of organized labor.

The enactment of the McNamara-O'Hara Service Contract Act on October 22 provided wage standards for employees performing work on Federal service contracts. These standards are similar to those long since applicable to employees on Federal construction and supply contracts.

Agricultural employers became subject to revised regulations governing applications for temporary foreign agricultural workers under the Immigration and Nationality Act of 1952 (Public Law 414). In addition to making a "reasonable effort" to recruit domestic workers, a grower was required to offer American workers wages varying by States from 90 cents to $1.25 an hour before foreign labor was permitted to be used. Beginning April 1, 1965, "nonadverse" higher wages—varying from $1.15 to $1.40 an hour—became effective. The revised regulations were issued after expiration of the Mexican farm labor program.

Social security amendments of 1965 included the so-called "Medicare" plan, which provided partial coverage for those over 65 for hospitalization, nursing home care, home nursing, and diagnostic expenses. An optional supplementary plan providing coverage for most major medical expenses was available for a $3-monthly premium. Benefits were to become available on July 1, 1966.

In November, the Industrial Union Department of the AFL–CIO arranged with 10 insurance companies to underwrite a pooled pension plan for employees of small companies. The program was available in 1966 for employers with fewer than 100 workers.

1966   The 6th biennial convention of the AFL-CIO, marking the 10th anniversary of the merger, convened in San Francisco on December 9. Retirements and resignations opened up eight vacancies on the Executive Council, which were filled so as to preserve the initial balance between former AFL and former CIO affiliates.

A pronounced upsurge in collective bargaining by public employee organizations became evident in 1966. One effect of this development was an increase in the number of strikes among public employees.

Two transportation strikes tested the adequacy of legislation designed to prevent work stoppages. New York City's transit system was shut down for 12 days, starting on January 1, in violation of a State law banning public employee strikes. Union leaders were subsequently jailed for violating a court injunction. Five major airlines were struck on July 8, after the Machinists rejected the recommendations of an emergency board. An agreement reached on July 29 and announced by the President on nationwide television was rejected by union members. A settlement was finally reached on August 19, when congressional intervention seemed imminent.

Farmworkers were successfully organized in California and Texas, with the movement for unionization extending eastward to Wisconsin and Michigan.

In August, the AFL-CIO chartered the United Farm Workers Organizing Committee to coordinate organizing attempts.

The 1966 amendments to the Fair Labor Standards Act, the most far-reaching in the history of the act, extended minimum wage protection to some 10 million workers previously excluded from the benefits of the law. The minimum wage for newly covered employees was set at $1 an hour effective February 1, 1967, with yearly increases of 15 cents an hour scheduled to boost the minimum to $1.60 an hour by February 1, 1971. The minimum wage for workers on large farms, covered for the first time, was not to increase beyond the $1.30 rate effective February 1, 1969. The amendments raised the minimum for workers previously covered by the act to $1.40 an hour effective February 1, 1967, and to $1.60 effective February 1, 1968.

Coalition bargaining, that is, the coordination of strategy and action among different unions having contracts with the same company, passed a major test when General Electric Co. negotiated a new agreement with the Electrical Workers (IUE) in the presence of representatives from 10 other unions.

After 34 years as president of the International Ladies' Garment Workers' Union, David Dubinsky, age 74, retired. He was succeeded by Louis Stulberg, secretary-treasurer.

Delegates representing the trade union movement in the U.S. walked out of the 50th session of the International Labor Conference, in Geneva, when a delegate from Communist Poland was elected as presiding officer. The boycott led to an open argument between Walter Reuther, who protested the action, and George Meany, who defended it, over the international program of the AFL–CIO

1967   Growth of collective bargaining in the public service, agriculture, and among professional workers, marked an active labor year. Man-days lost from strikes reached the highest level since 1959 as unions tried to recoup real wage losses caused by rising prices and sought reestablishment of wider wage differentials for skilled trades members. The Industrial Union Department continued to advocate coalition bargaining, which became an issue in the long copper strike.

Organizing gains among public employees were accompanied by increased strike activity and other forms of economic pressure. Teachers' strikes delayed the fall opening of public schools in New York City, Detroit, and other cities. In Federal Government, the number of exclusive recognitions continued to increase as the fifth anniversary of Executive Order 10988 approached. President Lyndon B. Johnson appointed a committee to review experience under Executive Order 10988, which constituted basic policy on employee-management relations in the Federal service, and to recommend changes in the Order.

Professional workers employed both their own independent associations and traditional trade unions during the year in increasing collective bargaining activity. AFL–CIO unions which organize professional workers moved towards closer cooperation. In March, they formed the AFL–CIO Council of Scientific, Professional, and Cultural Employees (SPACE), dedicated to enhancing organizing, collective bargaining, legislative, and public relations activities for the member organizations.

Labor organization continued among agricultural employees. Both the AFL–CIO's United Farm Workers Organizing Committee and the Teamsters union succeeded in obtaining new contracts with California growers.

After Teamster president James R. Hoffa began serving an 8-year prison sentence, leadership of the union passed to general vice-president Frank E. Fitzsimmons, whose first major test occurred soon after his election, in the national freight-hauling negotiations. The 3-year package was rejected by many steel-hauling truckdrivers, and a series of wildcat strikes continued for several weeks into the fall.

Early in the year, the unaffiliated Mine, Mill and Smelter Workers merged with the United Steelworkers. In mid-July, the merged unions and 25 others joined in a strike against major copper producers which continued through the remainder of the year.

A 5-man arbitration board, established by Congress in July after a 2-day railroad stoppage, imposed a 2-year settlement within the framework of previous bargaining on railroads and six shopcraft unions when the parties were unable to reach agreement within the time limits specified in the legislation.

A 3-year agreement calling for higher wages, a greatly increased supplemental unemployment benefit (SUB) plan, and other benefits ended a nationwide walkout at Ford Motor Co. which idled 160,000 auto workers for 7 weeks. Costs of the settlement were estimated at 90 cents an hour. Similar settlements were subsequently reached at General Motors and Chrysler without major shutdowns.

In its biennial convention in December, the AFL–CIO called for continued improvement in civil rights, increased consumer protection, and expanded public aid to education. The Federation explicitly rejected the application of guidepost formulas to collective bargaining and reiterated its support of double time as reimbursement for overtime. Earlier in the year, Auto Workers' president Walter P. Reuther and other top UAW officials resigned most of their AFL–CIO posts, protesting the "complacency" of the Federation's leadership.

1968   In January, the social security amendments of 1967 became effective, increasing benefits at least 13 percent and raising the payroll tax base from $6,600 to $7,800. Taxes were scheduled to rise to 4.8 percent in 1969, and by steps to 5.9 percent in 1987.

On June 12, the Age Discrimination in Employment Act (Public Law 90–202), signed by President Lyndon B. Johnson the previous December, went into effect. The act makes it illegal for employers, unions, and employment agencies in interstate commerce to discharge, refuse to hire, or otherwise discriminate against persons aged 40 to 65. On November 27, the Secretary of Labor, in response to a requirement under the statute, recommended that no changes be made in these age limits.

Congress passed Public Law 90-491 which gives Reservists and National Guardsmen new protection against discrimination in employment because of their military obligations or membership in the Reserves or National Guard.

Provisions restricting wage garnishment—the practice of attaching portions of a debtor's salary or wage for satisfaction of his creditors—are part of the Consumer Credit Protection ("Truth in Lending") Act of 1968. The anti-garnishment provisions were scheduled to go into effect July 1, 1970.

A major Fair Labor Standards Act case was decided by the Supreme Court in *Maryland* v. *Wirtz*. The Court held that coverage of employees of State and local government hospitals and schools was a valid exercise by the Congress of article 1, sec. 8 (the Commerce Clause) of the Constitution.

Union efforts to end racial discrimination and help the disadvantaged continued. The AFL-CIO created a new department to coordinate its urban rehabilitation programs, and pledged cooperation with business and government in placing the hard-core unemployed in jobs. The Federation's Building and Construction Trades Department announced a new program to facilitate non-white entry into trades apprenticeships. A number of AFL–CIO affiliated and independent unions also announced programs to aid underprivileged groups.

The United Mine Workers of America expelled its affiliate, District 50, in April, in a dispute over the latter's endorsement of atomic energy. The Mine Workers also initiated legal action to recover money loaned District 50, and to prevent use of the UMW name. The UMW and the Oil, Chemical and Atomic Workers later announced a plan for closer cooperation, stemming from recent oil company expansion into the coal industry.

In July, the Amalgamated Meat Cutters and Butcher Workmen of America and the United Packinghouse, Food and Allied Workers, with a combined membership of about 500,000, completed a merger. Another merger of the 60,000 member National Association of Post Office Mail Handlers, Watchmen, Messengers, and Group Leaders, and the 550,000 member Laborers' International Union of North America, was announced in April, but later difficulties and dissension within the Mailers' union created doubt regarding the finality of the action.

On June 14, I. W. Abel, president of the Steelworkers, was chosen president of the 5-million member Industrial Union Department (AFL–CIO) at a special meeting of the Department's Executive Board. He replaced Walter P. Reuther of the Auto Workers (UAW) who left the post after his union had been suspended by the AFL–CIO for dues delinquency.

Following a long series of policy disputes and an

earlier suspension, the United Automobile Workers formally disaffiliated from the AFL–CIO in July. The event marked the first major schism in the labor movement since 1957, when the AFL–CIO expelled the Teamsters and two other unions, charging corrupt practices. Shortly thereafter, the UAW and Teamsters formed the Alliance for Labor Action, to coordinate their efforts toward organizing, bargaining, community, and political goals. When other labor organizations were invited to join the new group, the AFL–CIO charged the two unions with attempting to set up a rival federation, and warned its affiliated unions that supporting or joining the ALA would be grounds for suspension. In November, following charges and counter charges of raiding, the ALA stated that it would be willing to enter into negotiations for a no-raiding pact with the Federation.

A bargaining settlement involving 400,000 Steelworkers and 11 major steel companies was reached in July, without a work stoppage or Federal intervention. In contrast, a 2-week nationwide telephone strike, the first in 20 years, occurred when the Communications Workers rejected company offers under a wage reopener clause. The long copper strike which had begun the previous July, was settled on a company-by-company basis, with the bulk of the workers finally returning to their jobs in late March, when the unions and larger copper producers came to terms.

Labor unrest among public employees, particularly in New York City, continued to mount. The city managed to avert a threatened transit strike, and to reach peaceful agreement with its non-uniformed employees (other than teachers), but experienced a 9-day garbage collectors' strike in February, a shorter strike by incinerator workers, and a bitter and prolonged walkout, beginning September 9, of its public school teachers over the issues of job security and school decentralization. The city and its teachers reached an uneasy truce on November 17. Teacher strikes also took place in Pittsburgh, Albuquerque, San Francisco, Hartford, and other cities. A 9-week garbage collectors' strike in Memphis ended shortly after the tragic death of Dr. Martin Luther King.

Leadership changes occurred in a number of national and international unions. A. Philip Randolph, long-time president of the Brotherhood of Sleeping Car Porters and outstanding spokesman for Negro civil rights, retired and was succeeded by C. L. Dellums. Charles Pillard became president of the International Brotherhood of Electrical Workers, replacing the retiring Gordon Freeman. James A. Suffridge, president of the Retail Clerks International Association also retired and was succeeded by James T. Housewright. Thomas E. Boyle replaced the late Walter L. Mitchell as head of the International Chemical Workers Union. David Selden was elected president of the American Federation of Teachers, replacing Charles Cogen.

George P. Shultz, dean of Chicago University's Graduate School of Business and a former professor of industrial relations, was designated Secretary of Labor on December 11 (sworn in on January 22, 1969).

1969   Effective January 1, 1969, 4 railroad brotherhoods —the Brotherhood of Railroad Trainmen, the Brotherhood of Locomotive Firemen and Enginemen, the Switchmen's Union of North America, and the Order of Railway Conductors and Brakemen—merged to form the United Transportation Union (AFL–CIO), having a combined membership of over 200,000. Charles Luna of the Trainmen became president of the new union. On the same date the 2,500 member

Railway Patrolmen's International Union merged with the 270,000 member Brotherhood of Railway, Airline, and Steamship Clerks. Later in the year the 2,000 member Railroad Yardmasters of North America (Ind.) merged with the 4,000 member Railroad Yardmasters of America (AFL–CIO). The latter's name and affiliation were retained.

The 8th biennial convention of the AFL–CIO, meeting in Atlantic City, N.J., October 2–8, expanded the number of vice-presidents on the Executive Council from 27 to 33. The delegates also voted to expel the 90,000 member Chemical Workers Union, which had joined the Alliance for Labor Action (considered by the AFL–CIO to be a rival federation) despite AFL–CIO warnings.

In December, the Bakery and Confectionery Workers, expelled from the AFL–CIO in 1957, returned to the Federation by merging with the American Bakery and Confectionery Workers' International Union (AFL-CIO).

The UAW-Teamster sponsored Alliance for Labor Action held its first convention in Washington, D.C., May 26–27. The nearly 500 delegates adopted a constitution and elected an executive committee, naming Walter P. Reuther and Frank E. Fitzsimmons as co-chairmen. The ALA resolved to "revitalize the labor movement," organize the unorganized, campaign for social and political action, tax reform, national health insurance, urban renewal, and cuts in military spending. Mr. Fitzsimmons was named Chairman of the ALA Organizing Committee. Work of the ALA was to be financed by a 10-cent levy from the monthly dues of 2,000,000 Teamsters and 1,600,000 UAW members.

The AFL-CIO established a Labor Studies Center, which began operation in September, to train union leaders in job-related technical skills and in the social sciences and the humanities. The Center is the first educational institution to be sponsored by the Federation. The Teamsters also announced establishment of a Labor Institute to train its local union officers and business agents.

In February, the AFL–CIO withdrew from the International Confederation of Free Trade Unions (ICFTU), in disapproval of ICFTU attitudes toward Soviet bloc nations and for ICFTU failure to comply with AFL–CIO demands to reject admission of the United Auto Workers to the world labor organization.

John L. Lewis, president emeritus of the United Mine Workers, who was instrumental in founding the Congress of Industrial Organizations and for many years was prominent in the American labor movement, died June 11, at age 89.

Effective February 1, an additional 1.5 million workers in the retail, service, hotel and motel industries came under the Fair Labor Standards Act; their minimum pay was set at $1.30 an hour, to be increased to $1.60 in 1971.

After expiration of an 80-day Taft-Hartley injunction on December 20, 1968, east coast dockworkers shut down major Atlantic and Gulf ports in a dispute over wages and benefits; "containerization" was a key issue. Settlement was reached in New York City, in mid-January, and strikes at other ports ended shortly afterward.

On October 27, the International Union of Electrical Workers (IUE), United Electrical Workers (UE), and other unions began a nationwide strike of General Electric plants.

The Department of Labor initiated systematic surveys of job openings in major cities, and proposed to establish computer job placement centers to facilitate placement of hard-core unemployed. The AFL–CIO announced strong 1968 gains in the apprenticing of minority members. A new USDL drive to open construction jobs to minorities began and focused first on the Philadelphia area. Builders were asked to submit specific minority hiring goals. The joint Department of Labor-National Alliance of Businessmen JOBS program announced expansion from 50 to 125 cities. The NAB reported in early 1969 that firms participating in JOBS had hired 120,000 hard-core unemployed. The program's goal is to hire 600,000 by May 1971.

On October 29, President Nixon issued Executive Order 11491, Labor-Management Relations in the Federal Service, which replaced Executive Order 10988, Employee-Management Cooperation in the Federal Service, issued by President Kennedy in January 1962. Among other changes, the new Order established a Federal Labor Relations Council to administer the program, and a Federal Service Impasse Panel to resolve disputes over new contract terms.

☆ U.S. GOVERNMENT PRINTING OFFICE: 1970 O—375–818